W9-CIP-865

5S for Healthcare

5S for Healthcare

Rona Consulting Group & Productivity Press

Thomas L. Jackson, Editor

CRC Press
Taylor & Francis Group
Boca Raton London New York

CRC Press is an imprint of the
Taylor & Francis Group, an **informa** business

A PRODUCTIVITY PRESS BOOK

Productivity Press
Taylor & Francis Group
270 Madison Avenue
New York, NY 10016

© 2009 by Taylor and Francis Group, LLC
Productivity Press is an imprint of Taylor & Francis Group, an Informa business

No claim to original U.S. Government works

Printed in the United States of America on acid-free paper
10 9 8 7 6 5 4 3 2 1

International Standard Book Number: 978-1-4398-0350-9 (Paperback)

This book contains information obtained from authentic and highly regarded sources. Reasonable efforts have been made to publish reliable data and information, but the author and publisher cannot assume responsibility for the validity of all materials or the consequences of their use. The authors and publishers have attempted to trace the copyright holders of all material reproduced in this publication and apologize to copyright holders if permission to publish in this form has not been obtained. If any copyright material has not been acknowledged please write and let us know so we may rectify in any future reprint.

Except as permitted under U.S. Copyright Law, no part of this book may be reprinted, reproduced, transmitted, or utilized in any form by any electronic, mechanical, or other means, now known or hereafter invented, including photocopying, microfilming, and recording, or in any information storage or retrieval system, without written permission from the publishers.

For permission to photocopy or use material electronically from this work, please access www.copyright.com (http://www.copyright.com/) or contact the Copyright Clearance Center, Inc. (CCC), 222 Rosewood Drive, Danvers, MA 01923, 978-750-8400. CCC is a not-for-profit organization that provides licenses and registration for a variety of users. For organizations that have been granted a photocopy license by the CCC, a separate system of payment has been arranged.

Trademark Notice: Product or corporate names may be trademarks or registered trademarks, and are used only for identification and explanation without intent to infringe.

Library of Congress Cataloging-in-Publication Data

Jackson, Thomas Lindsay, 1949-
   5S for healthcare / Thomas L. Jackson.
      p. ; cm. -- (Lean tools for healthcare)
   Includes index.
   ISBN 978-1-4398-0350-9 (pbk. : alk. paper)
   1. Health services administration. 2. Industrial productivity. I. Title. II. Title: Five S for healthcare. III. Series.
      [DNLM: 1. Health Facilities--organization & administration. 2. Efficiency, Organizational. 3. Quality Assurance, Health Care--methods. 4. Quality Control. W X 150 J14z 2010]

RA971.J33 2010
362.1068--dc22   2009031761

Visit the Taylor & Francis Web site at
http://www.taylorandfrancis.com

and the Productivity Press Web site at
http://www.productivitypress.com

Contents

Preface

In 2000, as the newly appointed president and CEO of Productivity, Inc., and Productivity Press, I had the honor of accepting, on behalf of the Productivity Development Team, the Shingo Prize for Productivity Press's successful *Shopfloor Series*. (President Bill Clinton once referred to the prize as "the Nobel Prize of manufacturing.") The *Shopfloor Series* presented the knowledge contained in Productivity's groundbreaking translations of Japanese quality and productivity manuals and case studies in a simple, intelligible format aimed at busy frontline workers and supervisors. The first book published in the *Shopfloor Series* was *5S for Operators*, which presented Japan's powerful 5S method of workplace organization to an entire generation of workers and managers.

This book, *5S for Healthcare*, restates the universal concepts and practices of *5S for Operators* in a language that speaks to healthcare providers and staff, and illustrates them with examples from cutting-edge healthcare organizations.

5S for Healthcare is intended to give you practical knowledge that you can use to make your healthcare organization cleaner and safer, and the job of providing quality care simpler, more satisfying, and more effective. It is about how to create a workplace that is clearly organized, free of clutter and chaos, arranged so you can find things, and sparkling clean—a place where patients are safe and anyone would be proud to work in. What you will learn about here is often called the "5S method," a reference to five words for the basic elements of this system: Sort, Set in Order, Shine, Standardize, and Sustain.* These activities are truly five pillars of an effective healthcare workplace. (This book uses 5S and five pillars as interchangeable terms.)

The 5S approach is simple and universal. 5S activities provide essential support for successful implementation of other important improvements in your organization, including lean healthcare (based on the Toyota Production System) and Six Sigma. More important, 5S can help healthcare organizations

---

* The original 5S terms were Japanese words that begin with "S."

maintain clean, safe conditions in the workplace so that facilities can easily pass the demanding accreditation surveys of the Joint Commission, DNV Healthcare* and state health departments.

Both *5S for Healthcare* and *5S for Operators* were developed from concepts in a longer book, *5 Pillars of the Visual Workplace*, written by Japanese manufacturing expert Hiroyuki Hirano. Although in many respects manufacturing and healthcare are worlds apart, in one respect at least, they are the same: frontline employees are the people who will be most involved in implementing the 5S approach. They are also the ones who—together with your patients— will benefit the most from it. We have developed this book specifically to give you the 5S basics in a straightforward format that healthcare providers and staff will find interesting and accessible.

5S for Healthcare presents an overview of the five pillars and devotes a separate chapter to each one. The first chapter of the book is like an "owner's manual," telling you how to get the most out of your reading by using margin assists, summaries, and other features to help you pull out what you need to know.

One of the most effective ways to use this book is to read and discuss it with other employees in group learning sessions. We have deliberately planned the book so that it can be used this way, with chunks of information that can be covered in a series of short sessions. Each chapter includes reflection questions to stimulate group discussion.

We hope this book will show you how easy it is to implement 5S and how you can apply it to make your workplace a better place in which to spend your time.

---

* On September 29, 2008, the Centers for Medicare and Medicaid Services (CMS) announced the approval of DNV Healthcare, Inc., as a deeming authority for U.S. hospitals. DNV is the first new organization to receive deeming authority in over 30 years. DNV has created a system that combines CMS conditions of participation with ISO 9001 quality management.

Acknowledgments

Productivity Press and the Rona Consulting Group would like to first acknowledge Hiroyuki Hirano for writing *5 Pillars of the Visual Workplace*, the book upon which *5S for Operators* is based. Mr. Hirano has formulated the concepts and tools of the 5S system in a way that makes them readily accessible to workforces and management teams of diverse organizations in industries throughout the world. Only a little effort has been required to transpose his original material from the context of manufacturing, where 5S originated, to the context of healthcare.

Second, we wish to acknowledge Park Nicollet Health Services, Signature Hospital Corporation, and Chugachmiut for providing the photographs of their 5S activities that illustrate these pages.

Third, we wish to thank Janice Midcap, Chris Dellinger, Marcella Will, Sally Strutzman, and my partner, Patti Crome, for providing important editorial feedback to ensure that the text of this book faithfully speaks the language of healthcare.

Fourth, we also would like to acknowledge the Productivity Development Team and many contributors, who first developed *5S for Operators*. In particular, Melanie Rubin, who assisted me on several major projects for clients, including Ford Motor Company, deserves credit for the inventive design of the **Shopfloor Series**, involving margin assists that speed the process of reading and comprehension.

Fifth, I personally wish to thank my partner, J. Michael Rona, for his foreword.

Finally, we wish to acknowledge the good work of the intrepid pioneers in the healthcare industry who are now in the process of implementing the 5S system in their own organizations. We welcome feedback about this book, as well as input about how we can continue to serve you in your 5S implementation efforts.

Tom Jackson, JD, MBA, PhD
Principal, Rona Consulting Group
Clinical Associate Professor
University of Washington for School of Public Health

Foreword

Most customers expect a perfect product when they purchase it. Most companies strive to produce zero defect products – they see it as good for customers and good for business. Those companies that excel at this focus on the highest possible quality at the lowest possible cost become great successes. Indeed, they see these two objectives as the 2 sides of the same coin. In order to produce this objective, these high performing companies have a management philosophy that serves as the foundation and methods and tools to ensure this result. They have known and published standards and processes and continuously strive to improve.

In healthcare, much of this focus, management philosophy and approach is haphazard and the result of luck. But, for some, this approach is beginning to gain some traction. After decades of trying to improve results by focusing on results, there are a handful of organizations that are taking a systematic approach to managing for excellence. These organizations are adopting the philosophy, management systems and improvement tools of Toyota and applying them to the processes of care for patients. The results, not surprisingly, are extraordinary for patients and for staff.

It is not unusual for healthcare to chase the latest improvement fad. For many, the Toyota Management System is another that they ought to be chasing. In this effort, they leap to methods rather than philosophy and select value streams and improvement events focused on the "squeaky wheel" problem. What most leaders do not understand is that after understanding the broad managerial system known as the Toyota Management System, the first step is 5S.

5S is the foundation of the Toyota Management System. It is the process that world class organizations tackle first. The reason for this is simple: an organization must be set in order before it can improve. What 5S does is ensure that the workplace is organized and properly ordered for good work to be performed. This includes the critical element of established Standard Work in place. Many of the improvement work that is done in healthcare today is actually documenting and putting in place – Standard Work. 5S ensures that the organization is ready for improvement, not wasting the time of people simply putting in formally, the way that work is done.

Dr. Jackson, in this book, reviews the principles, methods and tools of 5S for healthcare based on our experience over the last 9 years in healthcare. While staff do not always understand 5S and sometimes fear that it is just another management dictate, they find that the result is an orderly, more quiet, easier and more enjoyable environment in which to work. And, they find that it is much easier to make improvements afterwards.

5S, properly implemented, reduces the burden of bad processes on the staff member, increases staff satisfaction, increases customer satisfaction, reduces the 7 wastes of healthcare, creates cash and reduces cost.

A company truly committed to zero defects will first chase 5S with a passion.

J. Michael Rona
Principal – Rona Consulting Group

Chapter 1

Getting Started

CONTENTS

1.1 PURPOSE OF THIS BOOK

 5S for Healthcare was written to give you the information you need to participate in implementing the 5S method in a healthcare organization. As you already know, you are a valued member of your organization's team. Your knowledge, support, and participation are essential to the success of any major effort in your organization.

Figure 1.1 The book 5 *Pillars of the Visual Workplace*.

Key Point

The paragraph you have just read explains the purpose of this book. But why are you reading this book? This question is very important. *What you get out of this book largely depends on what you are trying to get out of it.*

You may be reading this book because your supervisor or manager has asked you to do so. Or you may be reading it because you think it will provide information that will help you in your work. By the time you finish Chapter 2, you will have a better idea of how the information in this book can help you make your job more satisfying and more efficient. You will also have a sense of how the 5S activities will make your workplace a safer, cleaner, and more pleasant place to work.

1.2 WHAT THIS BOOK IS BASED ON

This book is based on Japanese productivity expert Hiroyuki Hirano's definitive work on workplace organization, *5 Pillars of the Visual Workplace,* also published by Productivity Press (see Figure 1.1). It presents the main concepts and tools of Hirano's book in a shortened and simplified format that requires less time and effort to read than the original book. Although originally written for a manufacturing audience, Hirano's book is useful to healthcare providers and their organizations as a cross-reference for more detailed information on many subjects, including topics related to the design of a 5S implementation program.

1.3 TWO WAYS TO USE THIS BOOK

There are at least two ways to use this book: (1) as a reading material for a learning group or study group process within your organization and (2) for learning on your own. Your organization may decide instead to design its own learning group process based on *5S for Healthcare*. Or you may buy or be given this book to read on your own.

1.4 HOW TO GET THE MOST
OUT OF YOUR READING

1.4.1 Becoming Familiar with This Book

How-to Steps

There are a few steps you can follow to make it easier to absorb the information in this book (we have included a suggested amount of time for each step):

1. Scan the table of contents to see how this book is set up (1 minute).
2. Complete Chapter 1 for an overview of the book's contents (5 minutes).
3. Flip through the book to get a feel for its style, flow, and design. Notice how the chapters are structured and glance at the pictures (3 minutes).
4. Read Chapter 8, "Reflections and Conclusions," to get a sense of the book's direction (2 minutes).

1.4.2 How to Read Each Chapter

How-to Steps

For each chapter in this book, we suggest you follow these steps to get the most out of your reading:

1. Read the "Chapter Overview" on the first page (1 minute).
2. Flip through the chapter, looking at the way it is laid out (1 minute).
3. Ask yourself, "Based on what I've seen in this chapter so far, what questions do I have about the material?" (1 minute)
4. Read the chapter. How long this takes depends on what you already know about the content and what you are trying to get out of your reading. As you read:
   a. Use the margin assists to help you follow the flow of information.
   b. If the book is your own, highlight key information and answers to your questions about the material. If the book is not your own, take notes on a separate sheet of paper.
   c. Answer the "Take Five" questions in the text. These will help you absorb the information by reflecting on how you can implement it.
5. Finally, read "Summary" at the end of each chapter to confirm what you have learned. If you do not remember something in the summary, find that section in the chapter and review it (3 minutes).

1.4.3 Explanation of Reading Strategy

OVER
VIEW

These steps are based on two simple principles about the way your brain learns. First, as an analogy, it is difficult to build a house unless a framework is put in place. Similarly, it is difficult for your brain to absorb new information if it does not have a structure to place new information in.

Key Point

By getting an overview of the contents and then flipping through the materials, you give your brain a framework for the new information in this book. Within each chapter, you repeat this process on a smaller scale, by reading the main points, summary, and headings first.

Second, it is much easier to learn if you take it a layer at a time, instead of trying to absorb all the information at once. In terms of our house analogy, you can rarely paint a brand new wall with the first coat of paint. It is better to lay down a coat of primer, then one coat of finish paint, and later a final finish coat. When people read a book, they usually think they should start with the first word and read straight through until the end. This is not usually the best way to learn from a book. The method we have described here is easier, more fun, and more effective.

1.4.4 Using Margin Assists

As you have noticed by now, this book uses margin assists to help you follow the information in each chapter. There are eight types of margin assists.

Background Information	**INFO**	Sets the stage for what comes next
Overview	**VIEW**	Presents new information without the detail presented later
Definition		Explains how the author uses key terms
Key Point		Highlights important ideas to remember
New Tool		Helps you apply what you have learned
Example	**X**	Helps you understand the key points
How-to Steps		Gives you a set of direcions for using new tools
Principles	**P**	Explains how things work in a variety of situations

1.5 OVERVIEW OF THE CONTENTS

1.5.1 Chapter 1. Getting Started (pages 1–10)

This is the chapter you are reading now. It explains the purpose of this book and how it was written. It then gives you tips for getting the most out of your reading. Finally, it gives you an overview of each chapter.

1.5.2 Chapter 2. Introduction and Overview (pages 11–28)

There are five pillars in Hirano's system (5S) of workplace organization. Chapter 2 in *5S for Healthcare* starts by defining the word "pillar" and explaining why these five pillars are needed in an organization. It gives a short explanation of each of the five pillars. Then it describes some common types of resistance to implementing 5S activities. Finally, it reviews the benefits you and your organization will experience when the 5S program is implemented.

1.5.3 Chapter 3. The First Pillar: Sort (pages 29–46)

Chapter 3 introduces and defines the first pillar, *Sort*. It explains why the first pillar is important and describes problems that are avoided by implementing it. Then it explains the concepts, tools, and steps in the Red-Tagging Strategy, a technique used to implement the Sort pillar.

1.5.4 Chapter 4. The Second Pillar: Set in Order (pages 47–64)

Chapter 4 introduces and defines the second pillar, *Set in Order*. It explains why the second pillar is important and describes problems that are avoided by implementing it. Then it goes through the process of implementing the Set in Order pillar in an organization, describing the principles and techniques applied in each step. Some of the principles and techniques taught in this chapter include the following: the 5S Map, the Signboard Strategy, and the Painting Strategy.

1.5.5 Chapter 5. The Third Pillar: Shine (pages 65–80)

Chapter 5 introduces and defines the third pillar, *Shine*. It explains why the third pillar is important and describes problems that are avoided by implementing it. It explains how cleaning and inspection are related. Then it goes through the steps for implementing Shine in an organization, describing the tools and techniques taught in each step. Some of the tools and techniques taught in this chapter include the following: 5S Schedules, the Five-Minute Shine, and creating standards for Shine procedures.

1.5.6 Chapter 6. The Fourth Pillar: Standardize (pages 81–98)

Chapter 6 introduces and defines the fourth pillar, *Standardize*. It explains why the fourth pillar is important and describes problems that are avoided by implementing it. It also describes how the fourth pillar builds on the first three, creating standards for how the first three pillars will be implemented. This chapter goes through the steps for implementing the 5S pillar, Standardize, in an organization, and describes the tools and techniques applied in each step. Finally, it explains how Standardize can be taken to the higher level of prevention by applying techniques such as kitting and use elimination.

1.5.7 Chapter 7. The Fifth Pillar: Sustain (pages 99–111)

Chapter 7 introduces and defines the fifth pillar, *Sustain*. It explains how the first four pillars cannot be implemented successfully without the commitment to maintain them and describes problems that are avoided by implementing this fifth pillar. It discusses how an organization can create the conditions needed to implement the Sustain pillar and presents the role of healthcare management and professionals in maintaining commitment to 5S. Finally, this chapter describes a number of tools that an organization can use to sustain the implementation of the five pillars, such as 5S Slogans, 5S Posters, 5S Photo Exhibits and Storyboards, 5S Newsletters, 5S Pocket Manuals, 5S Department Tours, and 5S Months.

1.5.8 Chapter 8. Reflections and Conclusions (pages 113-120)

Chapter 8 presents reflections on and conclusions to this book. It discusses possibilities for applying what you have learned, suggests an approach to implementation in your organization, and suggests ways for you to create a personal five pillars action plan. It also describes opportunities for further learning about 5S implementation and lean healthcare (i.e., the application of the Toyota Production System to the management of healthcare processes).

Chapter 8 presents the conclusions to this book and suggests ways for you to create a personal 5S action plan.

SUMMARY

The purpose of this book is to give you the information you need to participate in 5S implementation in your organization. In order to get the most out of your reading experience, it is also important for you to ask yourself why you are reading this book.

You can read this book on your own or as part of a study group process within your organization. In order to get the most out of your reading, it is important to begin by familiarizing yourself with the contents, structure, and design of this book. Then you can follow specific steps for each chapter, which will make your reading more efficient, effective, and enjoyable. This strategy is based on two principles about the way your brain learns:

---

1. Your brain learns best when it has a framework in which to place new information.
2. It is easier to learn a layer at a time, instead of trying to absorb all the information at once.

Chapter 1, "Getting Started," is the chapter you have just completed. Chapter 2 defines the word "pillar," gives a short explanation of each of the five pillars of 5S, and reviews the benefits of 5S implementation. Chapters 3 through 7 explain the concepts and tools of implementing each of the five pillars: Sort, Set in Order, Shine, Standardize, and Sustain.

REFLECTIONS

Now that you have completed this chapter, take 5 minutes to think about these questions and to jot down your answers.

What did you learn from reading this chapter that stands out as being particularly useful or interesting to you in healthcare?

Do you have any questions about the topics presented in this chapter? If so, what are they?

Are there any special obstacles to implementing the 5S methods described in this chapter in a healthcare setting?

What information do you still need to fully understand the ideas presented?

How can you get this information?

Who do you need to involve in this process?

Chapter 2

Introduction and Overview

CONTENTS

2.1 INTRODUCTION TO THE FIVE PILLARS OF 5S

2.1.1 Context for Implementing the Five Pillars

 Healthcare facilities are like living organisms. The healthiest organisms move and change in a flexible relationship with their environment.

In the world of healthcare, patient needs are always changing, new healthcare technologies are continually being developed, and generation after generation of new medicines and medical procedures appear. Meanwhile, the pressure to improve the quality and reduce the cost of healthcare mounts each passing year. Because of these challenges, healthcare facilities must move beyond old organizational concepts and customs that no longer apply and adopt new methods that are appropriate to the times.

 Thorough implementation of the five pillars of 5S is the starting point in the development of improvement activities to ensure that healthcare is more accessible, more appropriate, and more affordable for all patients. In other words, the five pillars are the foundation for all activities aimed at improving productivity and flow, increasing quality, and reducing cost.

2.1.2 Overview of the Five Pillars

The word "pillar" is used as a metaphor to mean one of a group of structural elements that together supports a structural system. In this case, the five pillars are supporting a system for improvement in your organization.

Definition

Example

The five pillars are defined as *Sort, Set in Order, Shine, Standardize,* and *Sustain* (see Figure 2.1). Because these words begin with S, they are also referred to as the 5S's. The two most important elements are Sort and Set in Order. The success of improvement activities depends on them.

Imagine a healthcare facility filled with healthcare providers and support staff who do not mind working amid disorder, broken or misplaced equipment, and medical waste. People working in this healthcare facility consider the constant search for medical supplies and equipment as a normal part of their jobs.

These conditions indicate a healthcare facility that produces far too many clinical defects, where patients normally wait a long time for treatment, and where providers and support staff suffer from low productivity and morale. It is obvious that such a facility has failed to implement the Sort and Set in Order pillars.

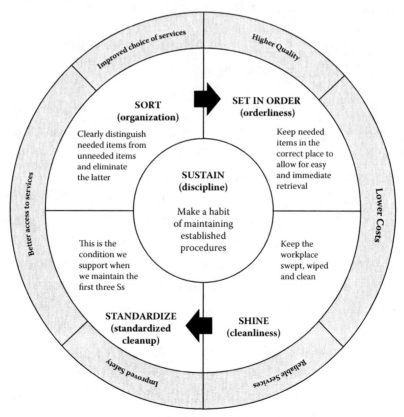

Figure 2.1 The five pillars.

Figure 2.2 A disorganized home environment.

2.1.3 Why the Five Pillars Are the Foundation of 5S Improvement Activities

As we said on the previous page, the five pillars are the foundation of improvement activities. When people first learn about the five pillars, it may be difficult for them to understand why. Here is an everyday explanation.

Example

People practice the five pillars in their personal lives without even noticing it. We practice Sort and Set in Order when we keep things such as wastebaskets, towels, and tissues in convenient and familiar places. When our home environment becomes crowded and disorganized, we tend to function less efficiently (see Figure 2.2).

Key Point

Few healthcare facilities are as standardized with five pillar (5S) routines as is the daily life of an orderly person. This is unfortunate since, in the daily work of a healthcare facility, just as in the daily life of a person, routines that maintain organization and orderliness are essential to a smooth, safe, and efficient flow of activities. Sort and Set in Order are

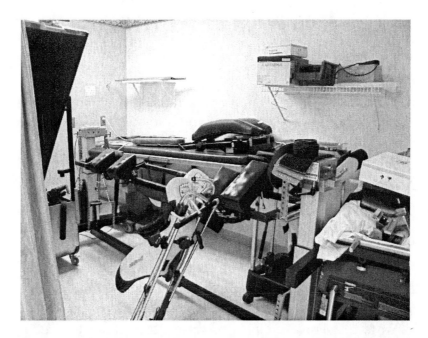

Figure 2.3 Storage in an operating room that needs the 5S system.

in fact the foundation for achieving cost reductions, safety improvements, zero defects, and zero accidents.

The 5S system sounds so simple that people often dismiss its importance (see Figure 2.3). However, the fact remains that a neat and clean healthcare facility

- Has higher productivity
- Produces fewer clinical defects
- Means patients do not wait so long for treatment
- Is a much safer place to work in

TAKE FIVE

Take 5 minutes to think about these questions and to jot down your answers:

- What are some of the quality, safety, and productivity issues that your organization is facing?
- What are some of the Sort, Set in Order, and Shine routines that are already part of your daily work life? Your daily personal life?

2.2 DESCRIPTION OF THE FIVE PILLARS

2.2.1 The First Pillar: Sort

Definition

Sort means that you remove all items from the workplace that are not needed for clinical and administrative processes and activities.

Surprisingly, this simple concept is easily misunderstood. At first, it may be difficult to distinguish between what is needed and what is not.

BACKGROUND INFO

In the beginning, getting rid of items in the workplace can be unnerving. People tend to hang on to all sorts of things, thinking that they may be needed for the next patient or procedure. In this way, equipment, medications, and supplies tend to accumulate and get in the way of everyday work. This leads to a massive buildup of waste throughout the facility (see Figures 2.4 and 2.5). In Chapter 3, you will learn to use a "red-tag holding area" to evaluate the necessity of an item instead of simply getting rid of it. This greatly reduces the risk of disposing of an item that might be needed later.

Example

2.2.1.1 Examples of Waste

The following types of waste lead to errors and clinical defects:

- Unneeded inventory creates extra inventory-related costs, such as storage space and management.
- Unneeded transportation of patients and supplies requires extra stretchers, extra linen, and supply carts.
- The larger the amount, the more difficult it is to sort out needed supplies from unneeded supplies.
- Large quantities of stocked items become outdated and obsolete due to limited shelf life.
- Clinical and administrative defects result from confusion created by unneeded in-process supplies and from equipment breakdowns.
- Unneeded equipment poses a daily obstacle to the flow of healthcare processes.

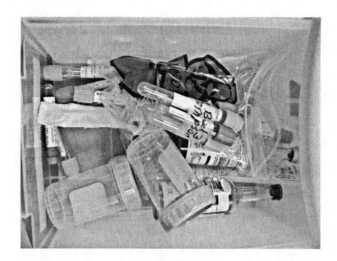

Figure 2.4 A messy pile of laboratory samples waiting to be processed.

Figure 2.5 Boxes of who-knows-what stored on the floor.

- The presence of unneeded items makes designing the layout of healthcare facilities and processes more difficult.

You will learn more about the first pillar, Sort, in Chapter 3.

2.2.2 The Second Pillar: Set in Order

Definition

Set in Order can be defined as arranging needed items so that they are easy to use and labeling them so that they are easy

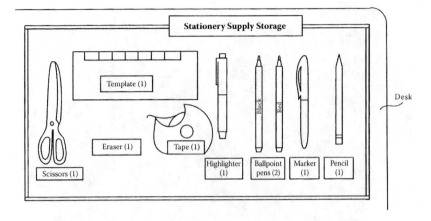

Figure 2.6 Example of Set in Order.

to find and put away. Set in Order should always be implemented with Sort. Once everything is sorted through, only
what you need to care for patients remains. Next, it should be
made clear where these things belong so that you can immediately understand where to find them and where to return
them. (See Figure 2.6 for an example of Set in Order.)

2.2.3 The Third Pillar: Shine

Definition

The third pillar is Shine. Shine means sweeping floors, wiping off work surfaces and equipment, and generally making
sure that everything in the healthcare facility stays clean all
the time, 24/7. In a healthcare organization, Shine can help
prevent the spread of hospital-acquired infections, such as
methicillin-resistant *Staphylococcus aureus* (MRSA).

Shine should be integrated into daily housekeeping tasks to
maintain safe environmental conditions as well as the proper
working condition of clinical and administrative equipment.

2.2.4 The Fourth Pillar: Standardize

Definition

Standardize differs from Sort, Set in Order, and Shine. These
first three pillars can be thought of as activities, as something
we do. In contrast, Standardize is the method you use to
maintain the first three pillars—Sort, Set in Order, and Shine.

It can also be an important method for keeping your facility ready for your next Joint Commission, DNV, or state health department accreditation survey.

Standardize is related to each of the first three pillars, but it relates most strongly to Shine. It results when keep equipment and work surfaces free of contaminants. It is the condition that exists after we have practiced Shine for some time.

2.2.5 The Fifth Pillar: Sustain

Definition

Within the context of the five pillars, Sustain means making a habit of properly maintaining correct procedures and environmental conditions. The first four pillars can be implemented without difficulty if the workplace is one where the employees commit to sustaining 5S conditions. Such a workplace is likely to enjoy high productivity and high quality. Such a workplace is likely to be safe for patients and providers alike.

Key Point

In many healthcare facilities, considerable amounts of time and effort are spent in vain on sorting and setting in order because the organization lacks the discipline to maintain 5S conditions and continue 5S implementation on a daily basis. Even if the organization occasionally organizes 5S campaigns and contests, without the Sustain pillar, the other pillars will not last long.

TAKE FIVE

Take 5 minutes to think about these steps and jot down your answers. Visualize your workplace:

- Think of one item you could get rid of.
- Think of one item you could relocate to use it more efficiently.
- Think of one item or area that would benefit from cleaning.
- Think of one regular routine you could create for getting rid of, relocating, or cleaning items in your work area.
- Think of some conditions you could create that would promote your carrying out this routine.

Resistance 1. Why Put Things Away or Clean When it s Not my Job?

Resistance 2. What's so Great about Sort and Set in Order?

Resistance 3. 5S Will Not Give Us More Time with Our Patients

Resistance 4. We Already Implemented Sort and Set in Order.

Resistance 5. We Did 5S Years Ago.

Resistance 6. We're Too Busy for 5S Activities.

Resistance 7. This is the Way We've Always Done It.

Figure 2.7   Common resistances to 5S implementation.

2.3 COMMON TYPES OF RESISTANCE TO 5S IMPLEMENTATION

2.3.1 Introduction

Key Point

Any organization introducing the five pillars of 5S is likely to encounter resistance (see Figure 2.7). Some common types of resistance are discussed below.

2.3.2 Resistance 1: Why Put Things Away or Clean When It's Not My Job?

Many healthcare providers are so busy—often as a result of searching for misplaced items in their disorganized work-places—that they have come to rely on the housekeeping or environmental services team to clean up at the end of the day. When 5S methods are introduced, people often say, "It's not my job to put things away or clean up." In fact, this negative attitude contributes to the disorder and sense of chaos that sometimes prevail in healthcare activities.

2.3.3 Resistance 2: What's So Great about Sort and Set in Order?

Sort and Set in Order seem so simple that it is hard to believe just how important and powerful they are! The fact remains that 5S implementation is needed when the healthcare facility is not neat, organized, and clean all the time.

2.3.4 Resistance 3: 5S Will Not Give Us More Time with Our Patients

Healthcare providers sometimes assume their job is simply to treat patients, not organize or clean things. This way of thinking is understandable if their job has never before included these functions. However, it is an attitude that needs to change as providers come to understand how important the Sort, Set in Order, and Shine activities are in ensuring patient safety, achieving zero defects, and reducing healthcare costs.

2.3.5 Resistance 4: We Already Implemented Sort and Set in Order

Some people consider only the superficial and visible aspects of the five pillars. They think that rearranging things a little and putting them into neat rows is all there is to it. However, such "orderliness" only scratches the surface of what the five pillars are all about.

2.3.6 Resistance 5: We Did Workplace Organization Years Ago

This type of comment is heard most often from people who think the five pillar movement is a fad. If they attempted workplace organization once 10 years ago, they do not see why they should do it again. The five pillars are not a passing fashion. They are the foundation for making all types of improvements.

2.3.7 Resistance 6: We're Too Busy for 5S Activities

In some workplaces, Sort, Set in Order, and Shine are the first things passed over when work gets busy. And in healthcare, work can get very, very busy. So, the explanation is that "we're too busy for that." It is true that work priorities are sometimes so pressing that other activities need to wait. However, 5S activities are as fundamental to healthcare as washing our face and brushing our teeth in our personal lives. We may be able to put these activities off for a short time, under certain circumstances. However, putting them off any longer quickly has negative consequences.

2.3.8 Resistance 7: This Is the Way We've Always Done It

If you tell people that it is more efficient to keep only one box of things on hand at each operation, they may respond by saying, "Yes, but we're doing all right, and this is the way we've always done it."

Key Point These types of resistance are common in the early stages of 5S implementation. If we ignore such resistance and plow ahead with implementation, the result is likely to be nothing more than superficial improvements. Instead, we need to address these concerns directly. In order for the five pillars to work, everyone needs to truly understand just how necessary they are to patient safety.

2.4 BENEFITS OF 5S IMPLEMENTATION

2.4.1 Benefits to Patients

Key Point So what can the implementation of the five pillars of 5S do for your patients? It should have many benefits for patients:

- A neat and clean healthcare facility produces fewer clinical defects.
- A neat and clean healthcare facility means patients do not wait so long for treatment.
- A neat and clean healthcare facility is cheaper to operate and helps reduce healthcare costs.
- A neat and clean healthcare facility promotes a sense of well-being that contributes to patient and provider morale.

2.4.2 Benefits to Providers and Staff

Key Point

So what can the implementation of the five pillars of 5S do for you as a healthcare provider or support staff member? It should have many benefits for you. It will

- Give you an opportunity to provide creative input regarding how your workplace should be organized and how your work should be done (see Figure 2.8)
- Make your workplace more pleasant to work in
- Make your job more satisfying
- Help you know what you are expected to do and when and where you are expected to do it
- Make it easier to communicate with everyone you work with

2.4.3 Benefits to Your Organization

Your organization will also experience many benefits from implementing the five pillars, such as raising quality, lowering costs, reducing the time patients wait for treatment, promot-

Figure 2.8   Providing creative input to workplace design.

Benefit 1. Zero Defects Bring Higher Quality

Benefit 2 . Zero Waste Brings Lower Costs

Benefit 3 . Zero Delays Means Patients Don't Wait

Benefit 4 . Zero Disorder Promotes Safety

Benefit 5 . Zero Abnormal Conditions Brings Better Process Availability

Benefit 6 . Zero Complaints Brings Greater Confidence and Trust

Benefit 7. Zero Blah Brings Lower Employee Turnover

Benefit 8. Zero Red Ink Brings Financial Stability

Figure 2.9   Benefits to your organization.

ing safety, building patient loyalty, and promoting financial growth for the organization (see Figure 2.9).

2.4.3.1 Benefit 1: Zero Defects Bring Higher Quality

Clinical defects result from many causes, including using the wrong medicine and treating the wrong patient. Sort and Set in Order prevent these types of errors. Furthermore, keeping equipment and the work environment clean reduces the amount of "walk time" spent searching for missing supplies. These and other effects of 5S implementation increase hours at the bedside and contribute to fewer clinical defects.

2.4.3.2 Benefit 2: Zero Waste Brings Lower Cost

Healthcare facilities and offices are storehouses of waste. 5S implementation can help eliminate the following types of waste:

- Excessive amounts of in-process supplies and supplies held in central storerooms
- Use of excessive amounts of space for storage
- Searching or waiting for medication or equipment that are hard to find
- Motion waste, in side-stepping poorly located equipment and supplies

Figure 2.10   Zero delays promote reliable deliveries.

2.4.3.3 Benefit 3: Zero Delays Mean Patients Don't Wait

In healthcare facilities that lack thorough 5S implementation, deadlines whiz by and patients wait while everyone is busy trying to remember what they did to the last patient, searching for equipment and supplies, waiting for doctors to make rounds, waiting for laboratory results ... the list goes on. It is difficult to keep patients from waiting in the face of problems such as wasteful motion and too many errors and clinical and administrative defects. When these problems are eliminated, processes become more reliable and patients are treated when they need to be seen (see Figure 2.10).

2.4.3.4 Benefit 4: Zero Disorder Promotes Safety

Injuries to patients or staff can be expected when equipment, medications, and supplies are left in hallways and when supplies are piled high in storage areas, or when work surfaces and equipment are covered with dust and other contaminants.

2.4.3.5 Benefit 5: Zero Abnormal Conditions Bring Better Process Availability

When daily maintenance tasks are integrated with daily cleaning tasks, providers notice problems in the process before they cause clinical defects and delays. In this way, work areas and equipment are more consistently ready for use. Clean, well-maintained work areas and equipment mean that processes break down less frequently and are easier to diagnose and repair when breakdowns do occur.

2.4.3.6 Benefit 6: Zero Complaints Bring Greater Confidence and Trust

Healthcare facilities that practice the five pillars are virtually free of clinical defects and delays. This means they are also free of patient complaints about the quality of treatment.

- Treatment in a neat and clean workplace is free of clinical and administrative defect.
- Treatment in a neat and clean workplace costs less to provide.
- Treatment in a neat and clean workplace occurs without making patients wait.
- Treatment in a neat and clean workplace is safe.

TAKE FIVE

Take 5 minutes to think about these questions and to jot down your answers:

- What are some of the benefits you might experience from 5S implementation in your workplace?
- What are some of the benefits that might be experienced throughout the organization from implementation of the 5S's?

2.4.3.7 Benefit 7: Improved Morale Lowers Employee Turnover

The five pillars of 5S can significantly improve employee morale. Studies have shown that healthcare providers who are more satisfied with their work environment are less likely to seek employment elsewhere. Considering that it costs, on average, much more than $80,000 to replace one registered nurse, this can have a very significant financial benefit for your organization.

2.4.3.8 Benefit 8: Zero Red Ink Brings Financial Stability

Healthcare organizations cannot make money without providing quality care or having the trust of patients. The five pillars provide a strong base upon which to build quality and patient trust and, in turn, loyalty. Therefore, healthcare facilities with a solid 5S foundation are more likely to become financially stable.

SUMMARY

The word "pillar" is used as a metaphor to mean one of a group of structural elements that together support a structural system. In this case, the five pillars of 5S are supporting a system for improvement in your organization.

The five pillars are Sort, Set in Order, Shine, Standardize, and Sustain. Thorough implementation of the five pillars is the starting point for improvement activities that will ensure quality, productivity, safety, and financial stability. This is because, in the daily work of a healthcare facility, just as in our daily lives, we perform routines that *sort*, *set in order*, and *shine*; these are essential to a smooth, safe, and efficient flow of activities.

Sort means removing from the workplace all items that are not needed for current activities. Set in Order means arranging needed items so that they are easy to use and labeling them so that they are easy to find and put away. Shine means sweeping floors, wiping off work surfaces and equipment, and generally making sure that everything in the healthcare facility

---

stays clean at all times, not just when the housekeeping/
environmental services team completes a scheduled cleaning. Standardize is the method for maintaining the first three
pillars. Sustain means making a habit of properly maintaining
correct procedures and environmental conditions.

When the five pillars are first implemented, it is inevitable
that certain types of resistance will arise. Some of these
include lack of understanding about why the five pillars are so
important, reluctance to clean since things will get contaminated again, and the belief that "it's not my job" because the
provider is too busy to take time out to organize, order, and
clean the workplace. This resistance can derail your organization's efforts at 5S implementation if it is not addressed
directly and carefully.

There are many benefits of implementing the five pillars
of 5S. The benefits to patients include reduced risk of injury
and being able to see providers when they want to, without
waiting. The benefits to providers include a more pleasant
workplace, greater job satisfaction, and an opportunity to
provide creative input to the way your work should be done.
The benefits to your organization include higher product quality, lower costs, increased patient satisfaction, lower turnover,
and financial stability.

REFLECTIONS

Now that you have completed this chapter, take 5 minutes to
think about these questions and to jot down your answers:

- What did you learn from reading this chapter that stands
  out as being particularly useful or interesting to you in
  healthcare?
- Do you have any questions about the topics presented in this chapter? If so, what are they?
- Are there any special obstacles to implementing the
  5S methods described in this chapter in a healthcare
  setting?
- What information do you still need to fully understand
  the ideas presented?
- How can you get this information?
- Who do you need to involve in this process?

Chapter 3

The First Pillar

Sort

CONTENTS

3.1 EXPLANATION OF THE FIRST PILLAR—SORT

3.1.1 Introduction

 We start learning early about getting things organized and sorted. As children, we were told to organize (sort) our toys and books. Strictly speaking, this type of organizing is not the same as that practiced as part of the five pillars. When children organize their toys and books, they usually line them up willy-nilly or store them jumbled together somewhere— without sorting out what is *necessary* (and to be kept) from what is *unnecessary* (and to be discarded).

3.1.2 Definition of the First Pillar

 Sort, the first pillar of the visual workplace, corresponds to the just-in time (JIT) principle of "only what is needed, only in the amounts needed, and only when it is needed." In other words, Sort means that you remove all items from the workplace that are not needed for current clinical or administrative processes and activities.

3.1.3 The Key to the First Pillar

 Sort does not mean that you throw out only items that you are sure you will never need. Neither does it mean that you simply arrange things into neat, straight patterns. If you really Sort, you leave only the bare essentials: When in doubt, throw it out. This principle is a key part of Sort in the context of the five pillars.

TAKE FIVE

Take 5 minutes to think about this question and jot down your answer:

- What problems occur in your work area because of the accumulation of unneeded equipment, medications, and supplies?

3.1.4 Why Sort Is Important

Key Point

Implementing this first pillar creates a work environment in which space, time, money, energy, and other resources can be managed and used most effectively. When the first pillar is well implemented, problems and interruptions in the workflow are reduced, communication between providers is improved, product quality is increased, productivity is enhanced, and the safety of patients and providers is improved.

3.1.5 Problems Avoided by Implementing Sort

When the first pillar is not well implemented, the following types of problems tend to arise:

1. The healthcare facility becomes increasingly chaotic and hard to work in.
2. Workstations, medication areas, shelves, and cabinets for storage of unneeded items put barriers between patients and providers, getting in the way of vital communication.
3. Time is wasted in searching for equipment, medications, and supplies.
4. Confusion about what is what and what goes where leads to clinical and administrative defects.
5. Unneeded equipment, medications, and supplies are costly to maintain.
6. Excess stock on hand hides other types of problems in activities.
7. Unneeded equipment, medications, and supplies make it more difficult to improve the process flow.

31

3.2 HOW TO IMPLEMENT SORT

3.2.1 Introduction

It is not always easy to identify unneeded equipment, medications, and supplies in a busy healthcare facility. Providers seldom know how to separate items needed for healthcare processes and procedures from unnecessary items. Healthcare managers and providers often look directly at waste without recognizing it.

New Tool

The red-tag strategy is a simple method for identifying potentially unneeded items in the healthcare facility, evaluating their usefulness, and dealing with them appropriately.

3.2.2 Overview of Red-Tagging

Red-tagging literally means putting red-colored paper tags on items in your healthcare facility that need to be evaluated as being necessary or unnecessary (see Figure 3.1). The red tags

Figure 3.1 Examples of red tagged items

catch people's attention because red is a color that stands out. An item with a red tag is asking three questions:

- Is this item needed?
- If it is needed, is it needed in this quantity?
- If it is needed, does it need to be located here?

Once these items are identified, they can be evaluated and dealt with appropriately. They may be

- Held in a "red-tag holding area" for a time to see whether they are needed
- Properly disposed of
- Relocated
- Left exactly where they are

3.2.3 Red-Tag Holding Areas

New Tool

In order to effectively implement the red-tag strategy, a red-tag holding area must be created. A red-tag holding area is an area set aside for use in storing red-tagged items that need further evaluation. This gives you a safety net between first questioning whether something is needed and actually getting rid of that item. This buffer is helpful when the need or frequency of need for that item is unknown or undocumented, which is very often the case.

Key Point

In other cases, the red-tag holding area can serve as an emotional buffer when people are concerned about getting rid of things. Sometimes we are concerned about giving up something we think we may need later. When an item is set aside and watched for an agreed-upon time, people tend to be more ready to let it go when that time is over.

3.2.4 Local versus Central Red-Tag Holding Areas

New Tool

Usually, an organization that is launching a red-tagging effort needs to establish a central red-tag holding area. This area is used to manage the flow of items that cannot or should not be disposed of by individual departments or work areas.

New Tool

Each department or work area that participates in red-tagging also needs a local red-tag holding area. The local red-tag holding area is used to manage the flow of red-tagged items within a local department or work area.

3.3 STEPS IN RED-TAGGING

3.3.1 Overview

How-to Steps

The red-tagging process in a department or work area can be broken down into seven steps:

Step 1: Launch the red-tag project.
Step 2: Identify the red-tag targets.
Step 3: Set red-tag criteria.
Step 4: Make red tags.
Step 5: Attach red tags.
Step 6: Evaluate red-tagged items.
Step 7: Document the results of red-tagging.

3.3.2 Step 1: Launch the Red-Tag Project

In general, red-tag campaigns are started and coordinated by the top management of an organization. When a red-tag campaign extends throughout the organization, local campaigns need to be organized in each department or activities area. This involves:

- Organizing a team
- Organizing supplies
- Organizing a time or schedule to perform red-tagging

- Setting aside a local red-tag holding area
- Planning for disposal of red-tagged items

3.3.2.1 Key Point

People from outside a department can be valuable members of a red-tagging team since they tend to see the area with a fresh eye. In particular, partnering with the materials management department in creating red-tagging teams helps with identifying and disposing of unneeded items. Of course, materials management is indispensable in setting new inventory par levels and reorder points, which helps prevent unnecessary inventories from accumulating in the first place.

3.3.3 Step 2: Identify Red-Tag Targets

Key Point Identifying red-tag targets means identifying two things (see Figure 3.2):

(a) Specific types of items to evaluate
In the work area, the targets for red tags include equipment, tools, supplies, and space. Inventories of medications and supplies can be divided into in-process inventories and inventories held in central storage areas.

(b) Physical areas where red-tagging will take place

Treatment	Description
Throw it away	Dispose of as waste or incinerate items that are useless or unneeded for any purpose.
Donate	Donate unneeded, outdated, or even expired items to charity organizations.
Sell	Sell off to other organizations items that are useless or unneeded for any purpose.
Return	Return items to the vendor for refund or credit.
Lend out	Lend items to other divisions or departments of your organization that can use them on a temporary basis.
Distribute	Distribute items to divisions or departments on a permanent basis.
Central red-tag area	Send items to the central red-tag holding area for redistribution, storage, or disposal.

Figure 3.2 Identifying red tag targets

It is better to define a smaller area and evaluate it well than to define a larger area and not be able to evaluate it fully in the time available.

TAKE FIVE

Take 5 minutes to think about these questions and jot down your answers:

- Name three types of items that you could target for red-tagging in your workplace.
- Name three physical areas in your workplace that could be targeted for red-tagging.

3.3.4 Step 3: Set Red-Tag Criteria

As we have already discussed, the most difficult thing about red-tagging is differentiating what is needed from what is not. This issue can be managed by establishing clear-cut criteria for what is needed in a particular area and what is not.

Key Point Three main factors determine whether an item is necessary. These factors are as follows:

- The usefulness of the item to perform the work at hand
  - If the item is not needed, it should be disposed of.
- The frequency with which the item is needed
  - If it is needed infrequently, it can be stored away from the work area.
- The urgency with which the item is needed
  - If the item is required in urgent care, it may need to be stored in the work area even if it is used only rarely.
- The quantity of the item needed to perform this work
  - If an item is needed in limited quantity, the *excess* can be disposed of or stored away from the work area.

In the final analysis, each organization must establish its own red-tagging criteria, and each department may customize this standard to meet its local needs.

3.3.5 Step 4: Make Red Tags

Key Point Each organization has specific needs for documenting and reporting the movement, use, and value of materials, equipment, medications, and supplies (see step 7 on page 41). The organization's red tags should be designed to support this documentation process. Various types of information on a red tag may include:

- *Category*—provides a general idea of the type of item (e.g., supplies or equipment)
- *Item name and reference or serial number*
- *Quantity*—indicates the number of items included under this red tag
- *Reasons*—describes why a red tag has been attached to this item
- *Division or department*—includes the name of the division or department responsible for managing the red-tagged item
- *Value*—includes the dollar value of the red-tagged item
- *Date*—includes the red-tagging date

The material used for red tags can be red paper, thick red tape, white paper with red ink, or whatever else works. Red tags can be laminated to protect them during repeated use. (See Figure 3.3 for an example of a red tag.)

3.3.6 Step 5: Attach the Red Tags

Key Point The best way to carry out red-tagging is to do the whole target area quickly—ideally, in a classic 5-day kaizen workshop. (See Figure 3.4 for an example of a typical kaizen week agenda.)

red tag

Category	1. Clinical equipment	6. Clerical equipment
(circle one)	2. Clinical tools	7. Clerical tools
	3. Medicines	8. Clerical supplies
	(4. Clinical supplies)	9. Clerical supplies
	5. Clinical documents	10. Other

Item name
Surgical gloves

Item No. *42*

Quantity	Value
500 pairs	*$2,000*

Reason	(1. Not needed)
	2. Defective
	3. Infrequently used
	4. Other

Disposal by: (department / division / section)
Central Red Tag Holding Area

Today's date:	Posting date:	Disposal date:
February 21, 2010	*February 28, 2010*	*March 30, 2010*

Red tag file no. *12345*

Figure 3.3   Example of a red tag.

The 5-day format of classic kaizen activity ensures that your improvement team will experience a complete cycle of organizational learning, thus increasing your chances of adhering to the new standards of workplace organization. Once your providers and staff have been trained and are comfortable with the methods and tools of 5S, red-tagging can be carried out in short and powerful 1- or 2-day events focused on very specific problem areas. At this stage in the game, you should

Day	General Content	5S Tools
Monday	Conduct training Gather data	Standardization Checklist (see Figure 6-X) Current 5S Map (see Figure 3-X) Red tags (see Figure 3-X)
Tuesday	Analyze data Brainstorm improvements	Future 5S Map (see Figures 4-6 and 4-7) Location Indicators (see Figure 4-X)
Wednesday	Trial improvements Make revisions	Visual Controls (See Figure 4-x) Signboards (see Figure 4-8)
Thursday	Execute improvements Write standards	Painting Strategy (see Photo 4-3) Cleaning/Inspection Checklist (see Table 5-1)
Friday	Report to management	

Figure 3.4   Typical kaizen week agenda for 5S

red-tag all items you question, without evaluating what to do with them. Refer to pages 42 and 43 in this chapter for tips on spotting unneeded items.

3.3.7 Step 6: Evaluate the Red-Tagged Items

Key Point

In this step, the red-tag criteria established in step 3 are used to evaluate what to do with red-tagged items. Options include the following:

- Keep the item where it is.
- Move the item to a new location in the work area.
- Store the item away from the work area.
- Hold the item in the local red-tag holding area for evaluation.
- Dispose of the item.

Disposal methods include (see Table 3.1) the following:

- Throw it away.
- Donate it to charity organizations.
- Sell it.
- Return it to the vendor for credit.
- Distribute it to a different part of the organization.
- Send it to the central red-tag holding area.

TABLE 3.1 Disposal Methods

Treatment	Description
Throw it away	Dispose of as waste or incinerate items that are useless or unneeded for any purpose.
Donate	Donate unneeded, outdated, or even expired items to charity organizations.
Sell	Sell off to other organizations items that are useless or unneeded for any purpose.
Return	Return items to the vendor for refund or credit.
Lend out	Lend items to other divisions or departments of your organization that can use them on a temporary basis.
Distribute	Distribute items to divisions or departments on a permanent basis.
Central red-tag area	Send items to the central red-tag holding area for redistribution, storage, or disposal.

Some unneeded, outdated, or even expired items some-times may be donated to charity organizations for ship-ment to developing countries, where medical equipment and supplies are frequently too expensive or difficult to obtain.

3.3.7.1 A Note about Large Equipment

As a target for red-tagging, equipment is as important as sup-plies. Ideally, unnecessary equipment should be removed from areas where daily work activities take place.

However, large equipment may be expensive to move. It is sometimes better to leave an equipment where it is unless it interferes with daily work or prevents workplace improvements. In the meantime, label unneeded equip-ment with a "freeze" red tag, which indicates that its use has been "frozen" but that it will remain in place for the time being.

3.3.8 Step 7: Document the Results of Red-Tagging

Key Point

As explained earlier, each organization has its own needs for documenting and reporting the movement, use, and value of equipment, medications, and supplies. Because of this, each organization needs to create its own system for logging and tracking necessary information as red-tagging takes place. The system may involve a written logbook in each department and in the central red-tag holding area. Or it may involve entering data from the red tags into a computer system.

Key Point

Whatever the system, documenting results is an important part of the red-tagging process. It allows the organization to measure the improvements and savings produced as a result of the red-tagging effort. As we indicated in step 4, your organization's red tags should be designed to support the documentation process it decides to use.

3.3.9 When Red-Tagging Is Completed

When red-tagging is completed, the facility is usually dotted with empty spaces and hallways are clear of obstructions—a sign of real progress and a real plus during a Joint Commission, DNV, or state health department accreditation survey. Now the layout of equipment and furniture can be changed to take advantage of the added space to promote the flow of work and patients. This is part of the second pillar, Set in Order.

TAKE FIVE

Take 5 minutes to think about this question and jot down your answer:

- What would be appropriate red-tagging criteria for your workplace? (Note: These criteria should address the three main factors of "need" for an item: usefulness, frequency of use, and quantity needed.)

Figure 3.5   Disorderly piles of operating room supplies.

Organizations that think they need to build a new health-care facility often discover plenty of space when they use the red-tag strategy.

3.4 ACCUMULATION OF UNNEEDED ITEMS

3.4.1 Introduction

Key Point Certain types of unneeded items tend to accumulate in work areas and storerooms in predictable places. This section gives some pointers about the types of unneeded items that accumulate and where these items are often found.

3.4.2 Types of Unneeded Items

Here are some types of unneeded items that tend to accumulate:

- Defective or excess quantities of instruments and supplies
- Outdated or broken equipment
- Outdated supplies
- Outdated surgical implants (very expensive!)
- Equipment, instruments, and supplies used by doctors who no longer work in the facility
- Obsolete computers and electrical equipment
- Outdated posters, signs, notices, and memos

3.4.3 Places Where Unneeded Items Accumulate

Here are some locations where unneeded items tend to accumulate:

- In rooms or areas not designated for any particular purpose
- In corners next to entrances, exits, or elevator lobbies
- Along interior and exterior walls, next to partitions, and behind pillars (see Figure 3.5)
- Under desks and shelves and in desk and cabinet drawers
- Near the bottom of tall stacks of items
- Behind computers, computer peripherals, and computer cables
- On unused management charts and bulletin boards
- In drawers and supply carts that are not clearly sorted

3.5 RED-TAGGING SUGGESTIONS AND REMINDERS

If done correctly, red-tagging can produce impressive results for your organization. To help you get the most out of your red-tagging efforts, we offer the following suggestions and reminders.

3.5.1 Apply One Red Tag per Item

When finding a shelf full of odds and ends, it is tempting to attach one red tag for the whole shelf. However, this can lead to confusion when it is time to dispose of these shelved items. Avoid this temptation and attach individual tags to individual items.

3.5.2 Red-Tag Excess Needed Items

We obviously want to red-tag items that are unneeded. However, we should also red-tag items that are needed if there are excessive amounts of them. Required amounts can be calculated based on the red-tagging criteria that have been set by the organization or the department (see step 3, page 36). Everything in excess of these amounts should be removed from the workplace.

SUMMARY

The first pillar is Sort, which means that you remove all items from the workplace that are not needed for current activities. When in doubt, throw it out. When the first pillar is well implemented, problems and interruptions in the workflow are reduced, communication between providers and patients is improved, defects are reduced, productivity is enhanced, and patients do not wait for care.

The red-tag strategy is a simple method for identifying potentially unneeded items in the workplace or in storerooms, evaluating whether they are needed, and dealing with them appropriately. To implement red-tagging effectively, a red-tag holding area must be created. A red-tag holding area is an area set aside for use in storing red-tagged items that need further evaluation. When an item is set aside and watched for an agreed-upon time, people tend to be more ready to let it go when that time is over.

Usually, an organization launching a red-tagging effort throughout the organization needs to establish a central red-tag holding area to manage the flow of items that cannot be disposed of by individual departments. Each department or

---

work area that participates in red-tagging also needs a local red-tag holding area to manage the flow of red-tagged items within the department or local activities area.

There are seven steps in the red-tagging process. Step 1 is launching the red-tagging project in the department or throughout the organization. Step 2 involves identifying red-tagging targets. This means identifying the types of items and the work areas to be evaluated. Step 3 is setting red-tagging criteria. There are three main factors in setting this set of criteria: the usefulness of the item to perform the work at hand, the frequency with which the item is needed, and the quantity of the item needed to perform the work. Step 4 is making the red tags. Red tags should be designed to support the organization's process for documenting and reporting red-tagging results. Step 5 is attaching the red tags. The best way to carry out red-tagging is to do the whole target area quickly—if possible, during a 5-day kaizen workshop. With more experience, small areas can be 5S'd in 1 or 2 days. Step 6 is evaluating red-tagged items. Here the red-tagging criteria are used to evaluate what to do with red-tagged items. Finally, in step 7, the results of red-tagging are documented. Each organization will have its own needs for documenting and reporting the movement, use, and value of equipment, medications, and supplies. Because of this, each organization needs to create its own system for logging and tracking red-tagging information.

When carrying out step 5, it is important to be on the alert for certain types of items that tend to accumulate in healthcare facilities and warehouses in predictable places. For your organization to get most out of its red-tagging efforts, it is also important to apply one red tag per item and tag excess amounts of needed items.

REFLECTIONS

Now that you have completed this chapter, take 5 minutes to think about these questions and jot down your answers:

- What did you learn from reading this chapter that stands out as being particularly useful or interesting to you in healthcare?
- Do you have any questions about the topics presented in this chapter? If so, what are they?
- Are there any special obstacles to implementing the 5S methods described in this chapter in a healthcare setting?
- What information do you still need to fully understand the ideas presented?
- How can you get this information?
- Who do you need to involve in this process?

Chapter 4

The Second Pillar

Set in Order

CONTENTS

4.1 EXPLANATION OF THE SECOND PILLAR—SET IN ORDER

4.1.1 Introduction

In Chapter 3 you learned about the first pillar, Sort. The second pillar, Set in Order, can be implemented only when the first pillar is in place. No matter how well you arrange items, Set in Order will have little impact if many of the items are unnecessary to providing the care your patients need. Similarly, if sorting is implemented without setting in order, it is much less effective. *Sort* and *Set* in Order work best when they are implemented together.

4.1.2 Definition of the Second Pillar

Set in Order means that you arrange needed items so that they are easy to use and label them so that providers and staff members—even employees new to your facility or work area—can find them and put them away when they are done.

4.1.3 Why Set in Order Is Important

Key Point

Setting in Order is important because it eliminates many types of wasteful clinical and administrative activities. These include the waste of endless searching for equipment, medications, and supplies; waste due to difficulty in transporting or using items; and waste due to difficulty in returning items to where they belong.

Example

Both clinical work areas and administrative offices have more than their share of searching waste. For example, it is not unusual to find in a hospital that nurses spend a great deal of their time looking for supplies, often making several trips to the storeroom before they find everything they need—for a single patient. Simply stocking frequently used items for the patient in cabinets can reduce the amount of walking nurses do by a factor of 10!

Example

4.1.4 Problems Avoided by Implementing Set in Order

The following list gives examples of the types of waste and the types of problems that are avoided when Set in Order activities are well implemented:

1. Motion Waste—The person sent to get a wheelchair walked all over the hospital to find one.
2. Searching Waste—No one can find the key to the locked cabinet that contains needed medications.

3. Waste of Human Energy—A frustrated provider gives up on finding a needed record after looking in vain for half an hour.

4. Waste of Excess Inventory—Desk drawers are crammed full of pencils, markers, and other stationery supplies. Outdated and obsolete supplies accumulate in storage areas.

5. Waste of Defects—The storage locations of two types of clear fluid are too close to each other and are not labeled, so the provider picks up the wrong fluid without noticing and injects it into the patient.

6. Waste of Unsafe Conditions—Equipment is left in a hallway, causing an ambulating patient to fall.

4.1.5 Definition of Standardization

Standardization means creating a consistent way of carrying out tasks and procedures. When we think "standardization," we should think "anyone." Clinical process standardization means anyone licensed to do so can administer care without creating defects. Equipment standardization means anyone licensed to do so can operate equipment without error. Standardization of supplies means that anyone can retrieve the right supplies easily.

4.1.6 Set in Order Is the Core of Standardization

Key Point

The Set in Order pillar is the core of standardization (see Figure 4.1). This is because the workplace must be orderly before any type of standardization can be implemented effectively.

4.1.7 The Concept of Visual Controls

Definition

Understanding where things are kept brings us to the concept of visual control. A visual control is any communication device used in the work environment that tells us at a glance how

Figure 4.1   Set in Order is the core of standardization.

work should be done. Visual controls are used to communicate information, such as where items belong (see Figure 4.2), how many items belong there, what the standard procedure is for doing something, the status of work in process, and many other types of information critical to the flow of healthcare activities.

Key Point   In any situation, we can implement standardization in such a way that all standards are identified by visual controls. When this happens, there is only one place to put each item, and we can tell right away whether a particular process is proceeding normally or abnormally.

In the Set in Order pillar, we use visual controls to communicate standards related to where equipment, medications, and supplies belong and how they are to be used. Be sure to notice how the methods described in the rest of this chapter use visual controls.

Figure 4.2 Visual control of a desk drawer.

TAKE FIVE

Take 5 minutes to think about these questions and jot down your answers.

- What are the three examples of visual controls that already exist in your workplace?
- Give one example of each type of waste listed in this section that you see in your workplace.

4.2 HOW TO IMPLEMENT SET IN ORDER

4.2.1 Introduction

How-to Steps

In this section, you will learn two steps to Set in Order.

- Step 1: You will learn some principles for deciding the best locations for equipment, medications, and supplies. Then you will learn a tool called the 5S Map, which is helpful in evaluating current locations and deciding best locations.

■ Step 2: You will learn how to visually identify these best locations once they have been decided.

4.2.2 Step 1: Deciding Appropriate Locations

The 5S Map takes you through a step-by-step process for evaluating current locations and deciding best locations. Before you begin learning about the 5S Map, however, it is important for you to learn some basic principles of why certain locations are better than others.

4.2.2.1 Principles of Storing Equipment, Medications, and Supplies to Eliminate Waste

BACKGROUND
INFO

The first set of principles applies to finding the best locations for medical equipment and instruments. These items differ from materials and things in that they must be put back after each use. However, some of these principles also apply to equipment, medications, and supplies. They say you should:

P

Principle

■ Locate items in the workplace according to their frequency of use.
  – Place frequently used items near the place of use (see Figure 4.3).

Figure 4.3   Commonly used items to be stored at the bedside.

- Store infrequently used items away from the place of use.

■ Store items together if they are used together, and store them in the sequence in which they are used.

■ If appropriate, preassemble instruments and supplies into kits. This approach involves gathering in one container all the instruments and supplies required to complete a clinical or administrative procedure, with zero setup.

■ Make storage places larger than the items stored there so that they are physically easy to remove and put back.

■ Eliminate the variety of equipment and instruments by establishing standards for the facility.

■ Store instruments according to function or procedure.

- Function-based storage means storing instruments and supplies together when they have similar functions. This works best for the emergency department or operating room or in other places where many procedures are normally performed.

- Procedure-based storage means storing instruments together when they are used on the same procedure. This works best for repetitive activities, such as surgery and laboratory or imaging procedures.

TAKE FIVE

Take 5 minutes to think about these questions and jot down your answers.

■ Identity two examples of how you could apply the principles of storing equipment, instruments, and supplies to eliminate waste in your own work.
■ Give one example of each type of waste listed in this section that you see in your workplace.

4.2.3 Using the 5S Map to Decide Locations

New Tool

The 5S Map is a tool that can be used to evaluate current locations of equipment, medications, and supplies, and to decide best locations. Using the 5S Map actually involves creating two maps—a "before" map and an "after" map. The "before" map shows the layout of equipment, medications, and supplies in the workplace before you apply Set in Order. The "after" map shows the layout of equipment, medications, and supplies in the workplace after you implement Set in Order. The "after" map will be discussed later in this chapter.

How-to Steps

The 5S Map can be used to evaluate orderliness in small or large work areas—for example, an individual workstation in the laboratory, a single operating room, or an entire nursing floor. Here are the steps to creating and using a 5S Map:

1. Make a floor plan or area diagram of the workspace you wish to study. Show the location of specific equipment, medications, and supplies.
2. Draw arrows on the plan showing the workflow between items in the workspace. There should be at least one arrow for every operation performed. Draw the arrows in the order that the activities are performed, and number them as you go (see Figure 4.4).
3. Look carefully at the resulting "spaghetti diagram." It is a "before" map that shows the workspace layout before Set in Order is implemented. Can you see places where there is obvious congestion in the workflow? According to the principles presented earlier in this chapter, can you see ways to eliminate waste?
4. Make a new 5S Map to experiment with a better layout for this workspace. Again, draw and number arrows to show the flow of activities performed.
5. Analyze the efficiency of this layout, using the principles we have already discussed.
6. Continue to experiment with possible layouts using the 5S Map until you find one you think will work well (see Figure 4.5).

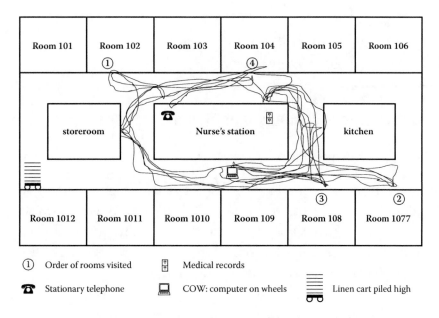

Figure 4.4　5S map of old layout for a nursing unit.

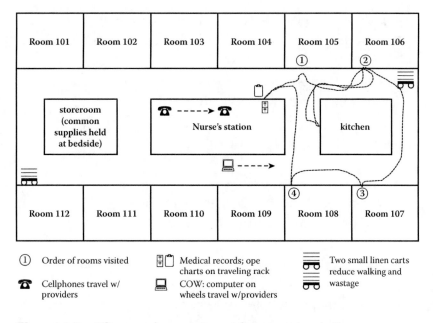

Figure 4.5　5S map of a new layout for a nursing unit.

7. Implement this new layout in the workspace, moving equipment, medications, and supplies to their new locations.
8. Continue to evaluate and improve the orderliness of the layout in the workspace.

4.2.4 Step 2: Visually Identifying Locations

4.2.4.1 Introduction

Key Point

Once best locations have been decided, we need a way to identify these locations visually so that everyone will know "at a glance" what goes where and how many pieces of each item belong in each location. We have several strategies for identifying what, where, and how many.

4.2.4.2 The Signage Strategy

New Tool

The Signage Strategy uses signs to identify what, where, and how many. The three main types of signage are:

- Location indicators, which show where items go
- Item indicators, which show what specific items go in those places
- Amount indicators, which show how many of these items belong there (see Figure 4.6)

Signage is also used to identify

- Names of work areas
- Locations of medications and supplies
- Equipment and instrument storage locations
- Standard procedures
- Equipment layout

Example

For example, a whole system of signage may be used in order to identify supplies stored on shelves in a central storeroom. Every section of shelving may have signs

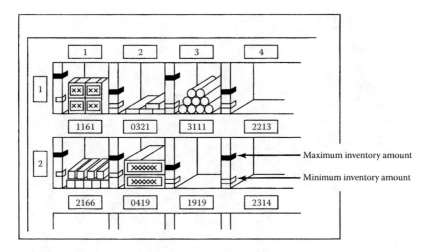

Figure 4.6 Amount indicators

identifying the section. Within that section, vertical and horizontal addresses on shelves can be identified with additional signage. Each item stored on the shelving may also have signage showing the "return address" for that item. The "return address" allows the item to be put back in the proper location once it has been removed (see Figure 4.7 and Figure 4.8).

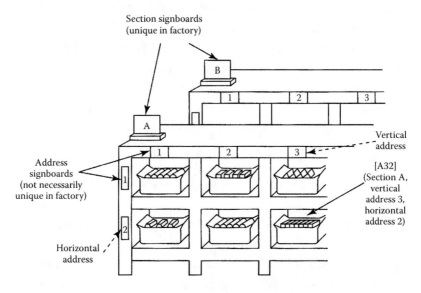

Figure 4.7 Addresses and return addresses for office tools.

Figure 4.8 Location indicators on shelving

4.2.4.3 The Painting Strategy

The Painting Strategy is a method for identifying locations on floors and hallways. It is called the "Painting Strategy" because paint is the material generally used. Plastic tape may also be used under certain circumstances, but it may fail to meet the Joint Commission's or your state health department's standards for cleanliness and hallway access. We suggest that tape be used only temporarily to *decide* locations through experimentation. Final locations should be *identified* with the Painting Strategy.

The Painting Strategy is used to create divider lines that mark off the healthcare facility's walking areas and hallways from its work areas. When mapping out hallways and work areas, we should keep certain factors in mind.

- In-process supplies should be positioned carefully for best workflow.
- If necessary, floors should be repaired before divider lines are laid down if possible.
- Hallways should allow for a smooth, safe flow of patients and equipment by being wide enough to meet regulatory requirements and avoiding twists and turns.

- Divider lines should be between 2 and 4 inches wide.
- Paint colors should be standardized, and the colors should be bright.

An example of a color standard is:

- Work areas are green.
- Hallways are fluorescent orange.
- Divider lines are yellow.
- Fire code demarcations are red.

Some types of divider lines include:

- Crash cart storage locations
- Aisle direction
- Door range, to show which way a door swings open
- Place markers for worktables
- Tiger marks (i.e., alternating yellow and black stripes), to show areas where inventory and equipment should not be placed or to show hazardous areas
- Red tape placed 18 inches from the ceiling to prevent stocked items on shelves from blocking sprinkler access

BACKGROUND
INFO The Joint Commission, DNV, and state health departments may frown on using tape—because it may harbor pathogens or other contaminants—as a permanent solution for executing the Painting Strategy. It is a good idea to use tape during a kaizen event to *decide* on locations and experiment with how well your decisions will work in practice. Plan to *execute* the Painting Strategy by replacing tape with paint once permanent locations are settled. For example, the equipment parking places in Figure 4.9 are outlined with tape during a kaizen event but later painted directly onto the floor.

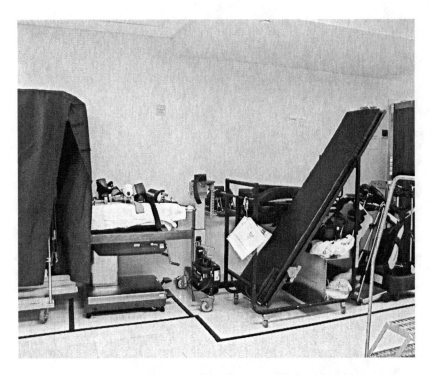

Figure 4.9 Parking places for operating room equipment.

TAKE FIVE

Take 5 minutes to think about these questions and jot down your answers:

- Give one example of how you could use the Signboard Strategy to implement Set in Order in your work area.
- Give one example of how you could use the Painting Strategy to implement Set in Order in your work area.

New Tool

4.2.4.4 The "After" 5S Map

The "After" 5S Map is a type of signboard. It shows the location of equipment, medications, and supplies in a given work area after Set in Order has been implemented. When posted in the work area, the "After" 5S Map is very effective in communicating the standard for where items are located.

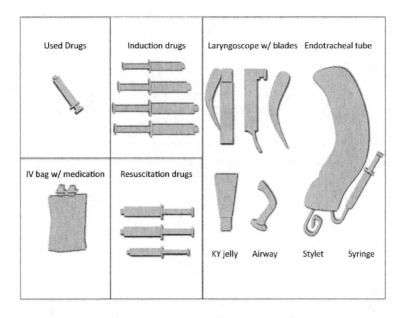

Figure 4.10 Example: Shadow board for an anesthesia cart.

New Tool

4.2.4.5 Color-Coding Strategy

Color-coding can be used to show clearly which equipment, medications, and supplies are to be used for which purpose. For example, if certain instruments and supplies are to be used to complete a particular medical procedure, they can all be color-coded with the same color and even stored in a location that is painted that color. Similarly, if different types of supplies are to be used on different equipment, the supply containers, medical waste containers, and equipment things can be color-coded to show what is used where.

New Tool

4.2.4.6 Shadow-Boarding Strategy

Shadow-boarding is a good way to show which equipment and instruments are stored where. Shadow-boarding simply means drawing and coloring in outlines of equipment and instruments in their proper storage positions. When you want to return a piece of equipment or an instrument, the outline creates a "shadow" of the instrument or piece of equipment and provides an additional indication of where it belongs (see Figure 4.10).

TAKE FIVE

Take 5 minutes to think about these questions and jot down your answers.

- Give one example of how you could use the Color-Coding Strategy to implement Set in Order in your work area.
- Give one example of how you could use the Shadow-Boarding Strategy to implement Set in Order in your work area.

SUMMARY

The second pillar of 5S is Set in Order, which means that items are arranged so that they are easy to find, to use, and to vput back. This is important because it eliminates many types of waste in clinical and administrative activities.

Standardization means creating a consistent way to carry out tasks and procedures. Another important reason to implement Set in Order is that orderliness is the core of standardization. The workplace must be orderly before standardization can be implemented effectively. Visual controls are devices used as you *set in order* to eliminate confusion about what is what by communicating the standards for how work should be done. *Visual setting in order* means using visual controls to implement Set in Order activities.

The first step in implementing Set in Order is to decide on appropriate locations. Two sets of principles are helpful in this decision: the principles of how to store, use, and replace equipment and instruments and the principles of motion economy. Properly locating equipment, instruments, and commonly used supplies—including medications and linen—can dramatically reduce walking and searching and increase efficiency.

The 5S Map is a tool that can be used to evaluate current locations of equipment, medications, and supplies and to decide best locations for these items based on the two sets of principles described in this chapter.

The second step is to visually identify best locations once they have been decided. The Signboard Strategy and the Painting Strategy are both used to identify what should go where and in what quantities. Other instruments for identifying best locations are the "After" 5S Map, the Color-Coding Strategy, and the Shadow-Boarding Strategy.

REFLECTIONS

Now that you have completed this chapter, take 5 minutes to think about these questions and jot down your answers.

- What did you learn from reading this chapter that stands out as being particularly useful or interesting to you in healthcare?
- Do you have any questions about the topics presented in this chapter? If so, what are they?
- Are there any special obstacles to implementing the 5S methods described in this chapter in a healthcare setting?
- What information do you still need to fully understand the ideas presented?
- How can you get this information?
- Who do you need to involve in this process?

Chapter 5

The Third Pillar

Shine

CONTENTS

5.1 EXPLANATION OF THE THIRD PILLAR—SHINE

5.1.1 Introduction

As you have learned in the last two chapters, implementing the five pillars begins when you Sort—getting rid of everything that is not needed in the workplace. This is followed by implementing Set in Order—putting the remaining needed items into order so that they can easily be found and used by anybody. But what good are sorting and setting in order if the workplace in which we function is not clean at all times and the equipment we depend on frequently breaks down? This is where the third pillar comes in.

5.1.2 Definition of the Third Pillar

Definition

The third pillar is Shine. It is the component that emphasizes the removal of dirt, trash, medical wastes, and other contaminants from the workplace. As such, Shine means that we keep everything wiped, swept, and clean at all times—not just once or twice a day when the housekeeping/environmental services teams complete a scheduled cleaning.

5.1.3 Why Shine Is Important

Key Point

One of the more obvious purposes of Shine is to turn the workplace into a clean, bright, safe, and sanitary place where everyone will enjoy working and patients are safe. Another key purpose is to keep everything in top condition so that when someone needs to use something, it is ready to be used. Many organizations have already abandoned the inadequate tradition of annual "year-end" or "spring" cleanings. Healthcare organizations in particular should go a step further and abandon the tradition that cleaning is something we pay housekeeping/environmental services teams or outside contractors to do. Instead, cleaning should become a deeply ingrained part of everyone's daily work habits, so that equipment, tools, work areas, and work surfaces will be ready for use all the time. (See Figure 5.1).

Cleanliness for healthcare facilities and offices is a lot like bathing for human beings (see Figure 5.2). It relieves stress and strain, removes sweat and contaminants, protects against infection, and prepares the body and mind for the next day. Both cleanliness and bathing are important for physical and mental health. Just as you would never consider bathing only once a year, performing Shine procedures in a healthcare facility should not be an annual activity. Just like washing your hands, Shine activities should happen constantly, throughout the day, and should be part of everyone's job.

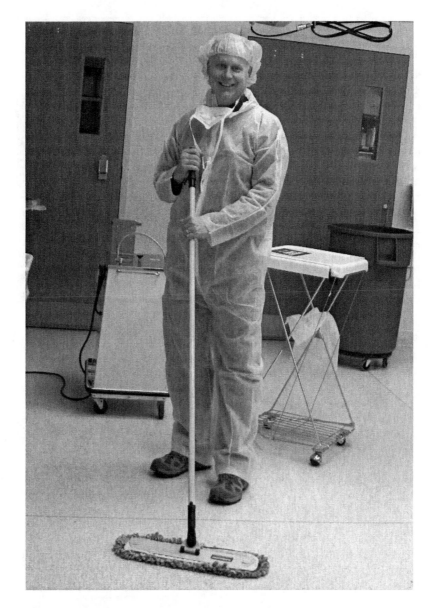

Figure 5.1   A doctor gladly helps with shine.

5.1.4 Problems Avoided by Implementing Shine

Shine activities can play an important part in aiding work efficiency and patient safety. Cleanliness is also tied in with the morale of employees and their awareness of improvements. Healthcare facilities that do not implement the Shine pillar suffer the following types of problems:

Figure 5.2 Shine activities relieve stress and strain.

1. Defects are more difficult to discover and correct in messy healthcare facilities.
2. Hospital-acquired infection rates rise when commonly touched surfaces are not cleaned constantly and hand washing is not a common practice.
3. Unclean work environments can lower morale.
4. Poorly placed equipment can cause falls.
5. Equipment do not receive sufficient check-up maintenance and tend to break down frequently.

5.1.5 Commonly Touched Surfaces

Key Point Pathogens are often transmitted through touch. This is the reason why hand-washing campaigns are a tool for controlling hospital-acquired infection rates. Shine activities can complement hand washing by identifying surfaces commonly touched by patients, their family members, providers, and staff, such as:

- door knobs
- beds
- chairs

Figure 5.3　Cleaning means inspection.

- TV remotes
- call buttons|charts
- night stands
- over-bed tables
- intravenous (IV) poles
- monitoring equipment

5.1.6 Cleaning Means Inspection

Key Point

When we clean an area, it is inevitable that we will also do some inspection of equipment and work environment conditions. Because of this, *cleaning also means inspection* (see Figure 5.3). This is another reason why cleaning is so important. We will talk more about inspection later in this chapter.

TAKE FIVE

Take 5 minutes to think about this question and jot down your answer.

- What are three types of problems in your work-place that could be avoided by implementing Shine procedures?

5.2 HOW TO IMPLEMENT SHINE

5.2.1 Planning Your Shine Campaign

5.2.1.1 Introduction

How-to Steps

Daily cleanliness achieved through Shine activities should be taught as a set of steps and rules that employees learn to maintain with discipline.

5.2.1.2 Step 1: Determine Shine Targets

Shine targets are grouped in three categories: stored items, equipment, and space.

- Stored items include supplies, instrument packs, and sterile trays.
- Equipment include laboratory instruments, monitoring equipment, crash carts, beds, desks, chairs, and computers.
- Space refers to commonly touched surfaces, floors, work areas, hallways, walls, pillars, ceilings, windows, shelves, closets, rooms, and lights.

5.2.1.3 Step 2: Determine Shine Assignments

Key Point

Workplace cleanliness is the responsibility of everyone who works there. First, we divide the healthcare facility into "Shine" areas. Then, we assign specific areas to individuals. Two tools we can use to do this are:

New Tool

- A 5S Assignment Map—One way to communicate Shine assignments is to mark them on a 5S Map. This 5S Assignment Map shows all the Shine areas and who is responsible for cleaning them. (Note: Do not leave any area without an owner. Assigning areas to housekeeping/environmental services teams does not count because they do not live with the process 24/7. (See Figure 5.4.)

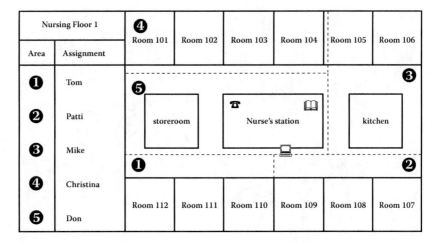

Figure 5.4 5S assignment map.

New Tool

- A 5S Schedule—This schedule shows in detail who is responsible for cleaning which areas on which days and times of the day. The 5S Schedule should be posted in the work area.

5.2.1.4 Step 3: Determine Shine Methods

Daily Shine activities should include inspection before the shift starts, activities that take place as the work is done, and activities that happen at the end of the shift. It is important to set aside times for these Shine activities so that they eventually become a natural part of the workday.

Determining Shine methods includes:

- Choosing targets and tools—Define what will be cleaned in each area and what supplies and equipment will be used.
- Performing the 5-Minute Shine—*Cleaning should be practiced daily and should not require a lot of time.* For example, much can be accomplished in 5 minutes of focused cleaning activity. We can assign specific tasks to each block of time devoted to Shine procedures, assuming that these tasks will be carried out efficiently (see Figure 5.5).

Figure 5.5 The 5-minute shine.

- Creating standards for Shine procedures—People need to know what procedures to follow in order to use their time efficiently. Otherwise, they are likely to spend most of their time getting ready to clean.

5.2.1.5 Step 4: Prepare Tools

Here we apply Set in Order to our cleaning tools, storing them in places where they are easy to find, use, and return.

5.2.1.6 Step 5: Start to Shine

Here are some suggestions about the implementation of Shine procedures:

- Be sure to sweep contaminants from floor cracks, from wall covers, and around pillars.
- Wipe off dirt, dust, and contaminants from commonly touched surfaces, including furniture, walls, windows, and doors.
- Be thorough about cleaning contaminants, medical waste, dust, and other foreign matter from all surfaces.

■ Use appropriate cleansing agents and disinfectants when wiping or sweeping is not enough to remove contaminants.

5.2.2 Ongoing Inspection and Maintenance of Cleanliness

5.2.2.1 The Need for Systematic Cleaning/Inspection

As we discussed earlier in this chapter, it is natural to do a certain amount of inspection while implementing Shine activities. Once daily cleaning and periodic major cleanups become a habit, we can start incorporating systematic inspection procedures into our Shine procedures. This turns "cleaning" into "cleaning/inspection."

Even when the workplace appears to be normal, pathogens constantly accumulate on commonly touched surfaces and contribute to hospital-acquired infections (see Figure 5.6). Patients (and their family members), providers, and staff constantly touch the surfaces of beds, chairs, call buttons, telephones, vending machines, and other commonly used

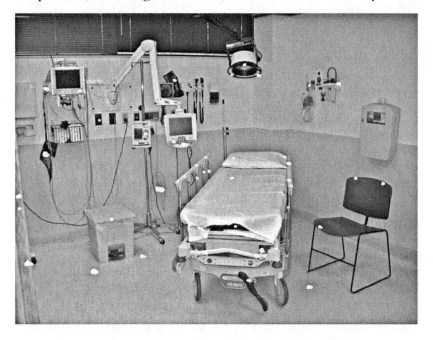

Figure 5.6 Target cleaning/inspection to prevent infection.

73

items. Healthcare providers on the front line—not the house-keeping/environmental services people—notice this first. It is important to take advantage of provider sensitivity toward the sources of hospital-acquired infections. Frequent cleaning/inspection can help locate and correct these problems.

5.2.3 Steps in Cleaning/Inspection

Key Point

The steps in cleaning/inspection parallel the steps in the Shine procedures but place greater emphasis on the maintenance of equipment and environmental conditions that are safe for providers and patients. These cleaning/inspection steps are listed below.

How-to Steps

5.2.3.1 Step 1: Determine Cleaning/Inspection Targets

The targets for cleaning/inspection are basically the same as the equipment-related targets noted earlier with regard to Shine duties. These include frequently touched surfaces, work areas, equipment, tools, and related supplies.

5.2.3.2 Step 2: Assign Cleanliness/Inspection Jobs

In principle, the people who carry out cleaning/inspection in a particular area or on particular equipment should be the same people who work in the area or operate the equipment. Depending on the complexity of the process or equipment, it is often a good idea also to involve supervisors and group leaders in cleaning/inspection duties.

New Tool

Once cleaning/inspection job assignments are determined, they should be written up (1) on a large signboard for the department or (2) on small signs attached to each target space or piece of equipment.

TAKE FIVE

Take 5 minutes to think about these questions and jot down
your answers.

- What types of procedures and schedules does your
  organization currently use to clean and inspect its
  work areas, equipment, and frequently touched
  surfaces?
- Who does the cleaning and inspection?
- What are some ways that your organization could
  involve healthcare providers more in cleaning and
  inspecting work areas and equipment?

5.2.3.3 Step 3: Determine Clean/Inspection Methods

Once cleaning/inspection targets and job assignments have
been determined, it is time to examine methods. First, list
all the inspection check items and combine them to make a
"Cleaning/Inspection Checklist." Table 5.1 shows an example
of part of a cleaning/inspection checklist.

5.2.3.4 Step 4: Implement Cleaning/Inspection

Key Point

When actually implementing cleaning/inspection, the key is
to use all your senses to detect abnormal conditions (i.e.,
conditions that are not standard to good quality, productivity,
and patient and provider safety). Inspection is not simply a
visual activity; it involves all five senses. Here are some tips to
diagnose environmental and equipment abnormalities:

- Watch how patients and their family members move
  through your environment to identify frequently
  touched surfaces that may harbor pathogens.
- Look closely at how equipment work and watch
  for slight defects (e.g., squeaking stretchers, sticky
  locks, IV poles that will not roll easily, wear, warp-
  ing, mold, missing items, lopsidedness, inclinations,
  color changes).

75

Table 5.1   Emergency Room Cleaning/Inspection Checklist

Zone 4 (Rooms 7, 8, 9, 10)

S1 Sort	Remove items from drawers that are not designated for said drawers
	Remove unnecessary items red-tagged and taken to red tag area
	Remove, tag, and put workorder in for any item not working correctly
	Eliminate safety hazards (no unexposed sharps, chairs out of walk-way)
	Remove items from cabinets that are not designated for said cabinets
	Remove all patient belongings after patient is discharged

S2 Set in Order	Return doppler, accucheck, clippers, medications to designated places
	Inspect that PAR levels are maintained
	Remove patient information from the vital sign machine after each patient use.
	Ensure reference materials are returned to proper labeled locations and neat

S3 Shine	Wipe cart, including rails, with sani-cloth prior to making cart
	Empty trash and take to dirty utility room
	Clean visible dirt and spills from floor and any equipment used, such as stands
	Wipe all telephones with sani-cloth
	Ensure visible signs are neat and appropriate

	1	2	3	4	5	6	7
	8	9	10	11	12	13	14
	15	16	17	18	19	20	21
month	22	23	24	25	26	27	28
	29	30	31				

5.2.3.5 Step 5: Correct Environmental and Equipment Problems

Key Point

All abnormal conditions related to the environment or to equipment should be fixed or improved. There are two approaches to corrective action (see Figure 5.8).

5.2.3.5.1 Instant Housekeeping

Whenever possible, a provider or support staff member should immediately fix or improve a problem he or she discovers during cleaning/inspection. This "instant housekeeping" requires that providers be trained and certified by infection control and housekeeping/environmental services teams so that they can handle countermeasures by themselves and immediately.

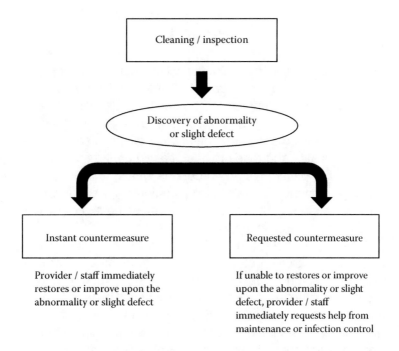

Figure 5.8 Two approaches for correcting problems.

5.2.3.5.2 Requested Housekeeping

In some cases, a provider or support staff member may determine that an infection control or housekeeping/environmental services problem is too difficult to handle alone or immediately. In this situation, the provider should attach a housekeeping/environmental services card to the site of the problem in order to flag the problem and make it visible. He or she should also request service from the housekeeping/environmental services department.

New Tool

It is also a good idea to log requested housekeeping/environmental services items onto a "Checklist of Needed Housekeeping/Environmental Activities." Once a requested housekeeping/environmental services item has been taken care of and its result is confirmed, the item should be checked off in the "confirmation" column of the checklist. The housekeeping/environmental services card should then be retrieved from the equipment where it is attached.

SUMMARY

The third pillar is Shine. Shine activities keep everything wiped down, swept, and clean at all times, not just when the housekeeping/environmental services team gets around to it. One of the key purposes of Shine is to keep all surfaces clean and equipment in top condition at all times so that they are always safe and ready to be used. When the third pillar is not well implemented, the problems that arise include poor employee morale, safety hazards, equipment breakdowns, and an increased number of defects, including higher rates of hospital-acquired infection.

There are five steps in implementing Shine in your workplace. These are (1) determining Shine targets, (2) determining Shine assignments, (3) determining Shine methods, (4) preparing Shine tools, and (5) implementing Shine. It is important to note that workplace cleanliness is the responsibility of everyone who works there, including providers, not just the infection control and housekeeping/environmental services staff. Two of the tools used in the implementation of Shine are 5S Schedules and the 5-Minute Shine.

Once daily cleaning and periodic major cleanups are a habit, systematic inspection can be incorporated into the Shine procedures. This turns "cleaning" into "cleaning/inspection." The steps of this inspection parallel the steps of the Shine procedure, but they place greater emphasis on the maintenance of work surfaces and equipment. These steps are:

Determine cleaning/inspection targets.
Assign cleaning/inspection jobs.
Determine cleaning/inspection methods.
Implement cleaning/inspection, using all your senses to detect abnormalities.
Correct environmental and equipment problems by correcting abnormal conditions immediately or making a formal request to the infection control or housekeeping/environmental services team to schedule needed cleanup or repair.

REFLECTIONS

Now that you have completed this chapter, take 5 minutes to think about these questions and jot down your answers:

- What did you learn from reading this chapter that stands out as being particularly useful or interesting to you in healthcare?
- Do you have any questions about the topics presented in this chapter? If so, what are they?
- Are there any special obstacles to implementing the 5S methods described in this chapter in a healthcare setting?
- What information do you still need to fully understand the ideas presented?
- How can you get this information?
- Who do you need to involve in this process?

Chapter 6

The Fourth Pillar

Standardize

CONTENTS

6.1 EXPLANATION OF THE FOURTH PILLAR—STANDARDIZE

6.1.1 Introduction

In Chapters 3, 4, and 5, you learned about Sort, Set in Order, and Shine. In this chapter, you will learn about a way to make sure the first three pillars are always implemented.

6.1.2 Definition of the Fourth Pillar

Standardize, the fourth pillar of our visual workplace, differs from Sort, Set in Order, and Shine. This is because it is the method you use to maintain the first three pillars.

In Chapter 4, we defined *standardization* as creating a consistent way to perform tasks and procedures. Building on this definition, we may define Standardize as the outcome when the first three pillars—Sort, Set in Order, and Shine—are properly maintained.

Example

6.1.3 Why Standardize Is Important

When you think about a city, you might say that a well-kept city block is one that has been swept and washed clean of dirt and debris. In the 5S context, a well-kept city block would be one in which the results of Sort, Set in Order, and Shine are maintained. This means that it would include only buildings, plantings, streets, and utilities that add to the beauty or function of the area, that these items are well laid out, and that the area is well maintained.

By contrast, a poorly kept city block might include broken-down or unused buildings, have no plantings, have inadequate utilities, and be dirty and unsightly.

In other words, Standardize integrates Sort, Set in Order, and Shine into a unified whole. After all, what good is the implementation of the first three pillars if conditions constantly deteriorate to what they were before implementation?

6.1.4 Problems Avoided by Implementing Standardize Activities

Here are some of the problems that result when we do not implement Standardize well:

- Conditions go back to their old undesirable levels even after a major 5S implementation campaign.
- At the end of the day, unneeded items are left from the day's work and lie scattered around the workplace.
- Tool storage areas become disorganized and must be put back in order at the end of the day.

- Sometimes contaminants and pathogens are not cleaned up immediately but are left to the housekeeping/environmental services team to clean up later.
- Even after implementing Sort and Set in Order, it does not take long for administrative staff to start accumulating more stationery supplies than they need.

Key Point

These problems and others reveal backsliding in gains made from implementing Sort, Set in Order, and Shine activities. The basic purposes of the Standardize pillar are to prevent setbacks in the first three pillars, to make implementing them a daily habit, and to make sure that all three pillars are maintained in their fully implemented state.

6.2 HOW TO IMPLEMENT STANDARDIZE

6.2.1 Making Sort, Set in Order, and Shine a Habit

6.2.1.1 Introduction

The three steps to making Sort, Set in Order, and Shine activities (the three pillars or 3S's) a habit are:

Step 1: Decide who is responsible for which activities with regard to maintaining 3S conditions.

Step 2: To prevent backsliding, integrate 3S maintenance duties into the regular work activities of providers and support staff.

Step 3: Check on how well 3S conditions are being maintained by providers and support staff.

We will discuss each of these in greater detail in the next section of this chapter. As you read this section, you will notice that some of the tools for implementing Standardize (such as the 5S Map) are familiar to you from your study of the Sort, Set in Order, and Shine pillars. This is because in order to standardize, we must use these same tools in a more systematic way to make sure that the first three pillars are maintained.

6.2.1.2 Step 1: Assign 3S Responsibilities

Key Point

When it comes to maintaining the 3S conditions, everyone must know exactly what they are responsible for doing and exactly when, where, and how to do it. If providers and support staff are not given clear 3S job assignments based on their own workplaces, the Sort, Set in Order, and Shine activities will not have much meaning.

Similarly, clear 3S instructions must be given to the people who deliver equipment and supplies from central storerooms or outside suppliers. Delivery sites and storage areas should be clearly marked and a 5S Map posted to show where equipment and supplies are to be stored. In each storage area, signage should make it clear whose things go where and in what amount. Materials management staff and outside suppliers should share responsibility with providers for maintaining 3S conditions in these storage areas and be encouraged to join in full 5S implementation.

Tools for assigning 3S responsibilities include the following:

New Tool

- 5S Maps (see Chapter 5, page 71)
- 5S Schedules (see Chapter 5, page 76)
- 5S Job Cycle Charts, which list the 5S jobs to be done in each area and set a frequency cycle for each job (see Figure 6.1)

In the example shown in Figure 6.1, 5S duties are sorted out according to the first three pillars and the scheduling cycle. In the figure, code letters are used for the various cycle periods: A is for "continuously," B for "daily," C for "nightly," D for "weekly," E for "monthly," and F for "occasionally." Each 5S job assignee can then use these charts as 5S Checklists. This particular example shows clearly who is responsible for each job, which area, what to do, and when to do it.

No.	5S Job Description	Sort	Set in Order	Shine	Standardize	Sustain	By shift	Daily	Weekly	Monthly	Quarterly	Annually
	5S Job Cycle Chart — Department: *Emergency Department* — Entered by: *Janice* — Date: *10-Feb-10*				S					Cycle Frequency		
1	Red-tag strategy (occasional, companywide)	0									0	
2	Red-tag strategy (repeated)	0				0						
3	Place indicators (check or make)		0						0			
4	Item indicators (check or make)		0						0			
5	Amount indicators (check or make)		0						0			
6	Sweep waiting area			0				0				
7	Sweep around nurses station			0				0				
8	Sweep under counters			0				0				
9	Sweep hallways			0				0				
10	Sweep clinical work areas			0				0				

Figure 6.1   Job cycle chart.

6.2.1.3 Step 2: Integrate 3S Duties into Regular Work Duties

Key Point

If providers and staff carry out 3S maintenance duties only when they see 3S conditions slipping, then a 5S implementation has not yet taken root. Maintenance must become a natural part of everyone's regular work duties. In other words, the five pillars—centered on maintaining 3S conditions—must be part of the normal workflow.

Visual 5S and 5-Minute 5S are two approaches that help make 5S maintenance work part of the everyday work routine for everyone involved in the process of providing care.

New Tool

6.2.1.3.1 Visual 5S

The Visual 5S approach makes the level of 5S conditions obvious at a glance. This is particularly helpful in healthcare facilities that handle a great variety and number of patients and procedures.

The main point of Visual 5S is that anyone should be able to distinguish between abnormal and normal conditions at a glance. This is especially important in healthcare, where failure to distinguish between the right medicines or instruments can too easily lead to injury or even death.

In Chapter 4, we defined visual controls as devices that tell us at a glance how work should be done. Clearly, the use of visual controls is central to the successful implementation of Visual 5S in healthcare, where we are focused on caring for the patient.

Example

6.2.1.3.2 The 5-Minute 5S

In Chapter 5, you learned about the 5-Minute Shine technique. The 5-Minute 5S is similar, but it covers all five pillars rather than just the third. When using the Visual 5S approach, instant visibility can act as a trigger for taking immediate 3S action (Sort, Set in Order, and Shine activities) against discovered abnormalities (i.e., disorder, contamination, and disrepair).

Key Point

We must also deal with the question of how skillfully and efficiently these actions are carried out. Instead of allowing 1 hour for preparing an operating room for the next patient or procedure, we can set up a half hour or "single digit" (i.e., less than 10 minutes) Shine procedure that accomplishes the same task. The term "5-Minute 5S" is a loose one—the actual time can be 3 minutes, 6 minutes, or whatever is appropriate. The point is to make the 5S work brief, efficient, and habitual. Figure 6.2 shows a signboard that was made as part of a 5-Minute 5S campaign.

6.2.1.4 Step 3: Check on 3S Maintenance Level

After we have assigned 3S jobs and have incorporated 3S maintenance into the everyday work routine of providers, we need to evaluate how well providers are maintaining the three pillars.

New Tool

For this, we can use a Standardization-Level Checklist. To evaluate the effectiveness of the maintenance activities, the evaluator ranks the Sort, Set in Order, and Shine levels on a scale of 1 to 5. Such a checklist can be made for specific department and/or activity processes. One example is shown in Figure 6.3.

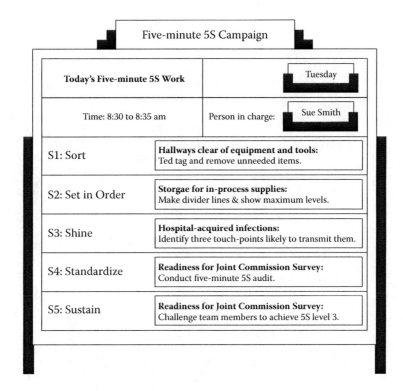

Figure 6.2 5-Minute 5S signboard.

Standardization-level Checklist		Assigned area:	*Nursing Floor 3B*	Date:	*15-Feb-10*
		Entered by:	*Janice Midcap*	Page:	*1 of 1*

No.	Process and Checkpoint	sort	set in order	shine	Total	Previous Total
1	*Room 301*				*8*	*6*
2	*Room 302*				*8*	*6*
3	*Room 303*				*6*	*5*
4	*Nurses Station*				*7*	*7*
5	*Storeroom*				*10*	*6*
6	*Lunch room*				*12*	*8*
7	*Average and total for 3B*	*26*	*28*	*28*	*50*	*38*

Figure 6.3 Standardization-level checklist.

5S Checklists, like the one shown in Figure 6.4, are used to check 5S levels in the organization as a whole. When an organization implements a 5S Month of intensive activities, 5S Checklists should be used to make weekly evaluations of 5S conditions.

The power of 5S Checklists in the healthcare setting is difficult to overstate. An organization that routinely maintains a

Location	Check Item	Check Description	1	2	3	4	5	T
Overall hospital	Are there clearly distinguished paths?	Are the clinical areas and paths clearly separated?	0	1	0	1	0	2
		Do providers and patients ever get in each other's way?	0	2	0	2	0	4
		Does the hospital use which and yellow lines to mark floor areas?	0	2	0	2	0	4
		Are there any exposed wires or pipes?	0	3	0	3	0	6
		Are there desks, shelves, or equipment jutting out into the paths?	1	3	1	3	1	9
		Are any boxes left lying around?	1	3	1	3	1	9
		Are there flowers or other ornaments in the hospital?	1	1	1	1	1	5
	Shelves and other	Are the item names and address shown on	0	2	0	2	1	5
			0	2	0	2	1	5

(Year and month: columns 1 2 3 4 5 T)

5S Checklist (for hospitals)

Hospital
Checked by:

Scoring: 3 = very good
2 = good
1 = OK
0 = not good

Location	Check Item	Check Description	1	2	3	4	5	T
Outdoors (overall)	Are there any unneeded items?	Outdoors (overall)	0	1	0	1	0	8
	Are storage areas clearly defined?	Areas for receptions, patient transfers, deliveries, storage, trash processing	0	2	0	2	0	8
		Have while and yellow lines been laid down?	0	2	0	2	0	4
		Are traffic signs used?	0	3	0	3	0	6
		Are there any exposed wires or pipes?	1	3	1	3	1	9
	Are outdoor areas kept clean?	Are trashcans, gardens, entrance areas, windows, and paths kept clean?	1	3	1	3	1	9
	Are there any unneeded items?	Are signboards, copy machines, and pathways arranged properly?	1	1	1	1	1	5
Clerical (overall)		Have fire-extinguishing equipment and emergency exits been established?	2	3	2	3	2	12
		Are floors clean?	0	1	0	1	0	2

(Year and month: columns 1 2 3 4 5 T)

8	8	8	8	8	8
8	8	8	8	8	8
2	2	2	2	2	2
5	5	5	5	5	5
5	5	5	5	5	5
5	5	5	5	5	5

Check Item	Check Description	1	2	3	4	5	T
	Are there any unneeded signs on the walls?	2	1	2	1	2	8
Restrooms	Are the names of meeting participants displayed?	2	1	2	1	2	8
	Are there any unneeded items?	0	1	0	1	0	2
	Are soap and paper towel dispensers kept stocked?	1	1	1	1	1	5
	Are the floor and sink areas kept clean?	1	1	1	1	1	5
	Is there any graffiti in the stalls?	1	1	1	1	1	5

Figure 6.4 5S Checklist for an entire hospital.

5S Level 2 is in a good position to pass a Joint Commission, or DNV, audit with few exceptions. An organization that routinely maintains a 5S Level 3 can probably pass a Joint Commission, DNV, or state health department accreditation survey with flying colors on any given day. At 5S Level 4 or 5, a Joint Commission, DNV, or state health department surveyor would learn a thing or two about best practices. We will explore this concept further when we discuss the concept of prevention.

TAKE FIVE

Take 5 minutes to think about these questions and jot down your answers:

- Identity one way in which Visual 5S could be used in your work area to help distinguish between normal and abnormal work conditions at a glance.
- Identity one 5-Minute 5S activity you could do daily that would improve the efficiency of your work.

6.2.2 Taking It to the Next Level: Prevention

BACKGROUND
INFO 6.2.2.1 The Concept of Prevention

Key Point

When we find that equipment or instruments have not been put back correctly, we immediately take care of them. When we find medical waste on a work surface, we immediately clean it up. We do not wait for the housekeeping/environmental services team to do it later. Making these actions habitual is the foundation of Standardize. However, when the same problems keep happening over and over again, it is time to take the concept of Standardize to the next level: prevention.

To take this pillar to a higher level, we must ask, "Why?" Why do unneeded items accumulate (despite Sort procedures)? Why do equipment, medications, and supplies get put back incorrectly (despite Set in Order procedures)? Why do work surfaces and equipment become contaminated (despite Shine procedures)? When we ask "why" repeatedly, we eventually find the source of the problem and can address that source with a fundamental improvement. Such improvements can help us develop *Unbreakable Standardization* (see Figure 6.5), which means:

Definition

- Unbreakable Sorting
- Unbreakable Setting in Order
- Unbreakable Shining

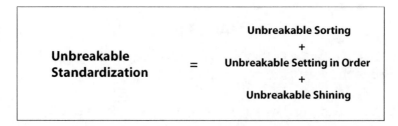

Figure 6.5   Unbreakable standardization.

6.2.2.2 Prevent Unneeded Items from Accumulating (Preventive Sort Procedures)

The Red-Tag Strategy described in Chapter 3 is our main means of sorting out unneeded items. This strategy is a visual control method that enables anyone to see at a glance which items are no longer needed. However, we should note that the Red-Tag Strategy is an after-the-fact approach that deals with unneeded items that have accumulated. No matter how often we implement this strategy, unneeded items will accumulate in the interim.

Definition

Nowadays, smart organizations are shifting from this type of "after-the-fact" sorting to preventive sorting. Preventive sorting means that instead of waiting until unneeded items accumulate, we find ways to prevent their accumulation. We could also call this approach "unbreakable" sorting because once Sort procedures have been implemented, having only needed items in the workplace becomes an "unbreakable" condition.

Key Point

To achieve unbreakable sorting, we must prevent unneeded items from even entering the workplace. To prevent the accumulation of unneeded equipment and supplies, we must find a way to procure and store only those items that are needed, only when they are needed, and only in the amount needed.

For example, suppose your organization is scheduled to carry out a certain number of medical procedures in a particular month. Ideally, at the beginning of this month, only the things needed to complete the scheduled number of procedures would be delivered to you from your materials management or directly from external suppliers. For any given procedure, your organization might even receive the necessary supplies in small, more frequent deliveries, depending on the type of procedure and the delivery and storage considerations.

Receiving things just in time for activities rather than storing large quantities of things in advance eliminates many of the potential costs associated with maintaining supplies, including expensive surgical implants. As well, receiving things just in time is a preventive measure that avoids the accumulation of things that need to be sorted, which can easily lead to misidentification errors and potentially catastrophic defects.

Definition

6.2.2.3 Prevent Things from Getting Mixed Up (Preventive Set in Order Procedures)

Key Point

Preventive setting in order means keeping Set in Order procedures from breaking down. To achieve preventive setting in order, we must somehow prevent the inefficiency that results from the lack of orderly control of any specific item. There are two ways to do this: (1) make it difficult to put things in the wrong place and (2) make it impossible to put things in the wrong place.

The first method relies heavily on discipline and visual controls. Clearly marked storage areas show at a glance what goes where and in what amount. When it is obvious what goes where and in what amount, it is difficult to mix things up. This condition supports setting in order that is difficult to break. Figure 6.6 shows how a simple rack prevents the highly dangerous mix-up of laboratory samples in an emergency department. The samples for a single patient are stored in a single row corresponding to the patient's room number instead of being tossed together into a bin (see Figure 2.2 on page 14). A similar approach can be taken to encourage providers and staff to return instruments and equipment to their proper storage places, so that they will be available for use the next time they are needed.

However, there is still a big difference between setting in order that is difficult to break and setting in order that is unbreakable. Why settle for the first when the second is possible? But how do we achieve unbreakable setting in order?

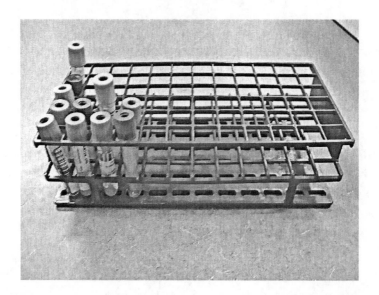

Figure 6.6 A mistake-proof rack prevents mix-ups of laboratory samples.

6.2.2.4 The Five Why's and One How (5W1H) Approach

New Tool

We begin by asking, "Why?" until we identify the underlying causes—for every answer we get, we must ask, "Why?" again. Usually, we ask, "Why?" at least five times to get to the root of the problem. When we do find the underlying cause, we ask, "How" we can fix it. Accordingly, this method is called the "5W1H" approach.

Key Point

When we ask why setting in order is breakable, we find that one answer is because people make mistakes putting things back. At this point, we need to identify what types of items are not being returned correctly. Once we identify this, the question is how to achieve unbreakable setting in order by making it impossible to return them to the wrong place. If we can somehow eliminate the need to return items at all, we can achieve unbreakable setting in order. Three techniques for doing this are kitting, incorporation, and use elimination.

6.2.2.5 Kitting

New Tool

In the kitting technique, equipment, instruments, and supplies are preassembled in a "kit" to prevent the need for searching

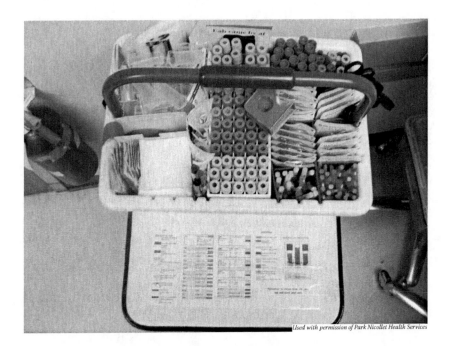

Used with permission of Park Nicollet Health Services

Figure 6.7 Example of a blood draw kit.

and retrieving equipment, instruments, and supplies before beginning work. We are familiar with kitting in the operating room and the emergency department, but kitting has many other potential applications in healthcare. Figure 6.7 shows this method in practice in the process of drawing blood.

Although this technique does not eliminate the need to pre-assemble items, it does effectively eliminate the need for providers to search for them over and over again. We can frequently rely on trained support staff to create kits, freeing providers to serve patients and eliminate unnecessary delays in treatment. This technique achieves unbreakable Setting in Order.

6.2.2.6 Incorporation

New Tool

Incorporation means creating a flow of services in a health-care facility process in which

- Equipment, medications, and supplies are smoothly integrated into the process

93

Figure 6.8 Example of incorporation in a post-operative acute care unit.

■ Equipment, medications, and supplies are stored where they are used and therefore do not have to be returned after use

Figure 6.8 shows an example of a supply cabinet stocked with items commonly used by nurses when making their rounds in the hospital. Such cabinets have been installed in virtually all patient rooms and are restocked daily. Incorporating storage into the workflow has eliminated the need for frequent visits to the central storeroom, eliminated thousands of miles of walking throughout the year, and permitted nurses to spend more time with their patients.

New Tool

Key Point

6.2.2.7 Use Elimination

Kitting and incorporating equipment, medications, and supplies effectively eliminate the need to retrieve or return them after each use. However, these items are still being used, requiring energy to organize them in the first place.

The question is whether there is some way to serve the function of the tool without using the equipment, instruments, or supplies. A Set in Order approach that eliminates the use of particular equipment, instruments, or supplies is in fact unbreakable setting in order.

Stretch yourself by thinking about the following three techniques for eliminating the use of certain equipment, medications, and supplies.

6.2.2.7.1 Tool Unification

Definition

Tool unification means combining the functions of two or more instruments or pieces of equipment into a single tool. It is an approach that usually reaches back to the design stage. For example, consider the integration of an EKG monitor with a pulse oximetry module.

6.2.2.7.2 Tool Substitution

Definition

Tool substitution means using something other than a tool to serve the tool's function, thereby eliminating the tool. For example,

- Prefilled syringes (eliminates bottles)
- Prelabeled syringes (eliminates labels)
- Computer documentation (eliminates paper charts)

TAKE FIVE

Take 5 minutes to think about these questions and jot down your answers:

- Give one example each of how kitting, incorporation, and use elimination could make it unnecessary to return specific items in your work area.
- Give one example of how you could prevent unneeded items from accumulating in your work area.

Definition

6.2.2.8 Prevent Contamination (Preventive Shine Method)

Key Point

Preventive Shine Methods will prevent things from getting contaminated to begin with. Anyone who has participated in

Ordinary fingernail clippers scatter clippings   Fingernail clippers with Cleanliness device

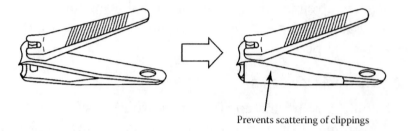

Prevents scattering of clippings

Figure 6.9 A nail clipper that incorporates prevention.

5S implementation can tell you that the initial cleanup is very hard work. The key to minimizing the drudgery of cleaning up is to treat contamination problems at their source. The 5 Why's approach can be applied to figure out why contaminants are being generated and how this problem can be fixed. In Figure 6.9, we see how the design of a simple nail clipper has been improved to contain nail clippings, rather than letting them fall on the floor.

In Figure 6.10, we see individually wrapped stirring sticks for coffee have replaced unwrapped stirring sticks for coffee in the emergency department waiting room. This prevents incoming patients and their family members from inadvertently transmitting potentially dangerous pathogens to other patients and their families. The closer you can get to the source of the contamination, the better you will be able to standardize procedures.

TAKE FIVE

Take 5 minutes to think about this question and jot down your answer:

- Give one example of how the 5 Why's technique could help identify the cause of a cleanliness problem in your work area.

Figure 6.10   Example of prevention in the waiting room.

SUMMARY

The fourth pillar is Standardize, which is the result of properly maintaining the first three pillars—Sort, Set in Order, and Shine. The basic purposes of Standardize are to prevent setbacks in the first three pillars, to make them a daily habit, and to make sure they are maintained in their fully implemented state.

The first part of implementing the fourth pillar involves making Sort, Set in Order, and Shine a habit. The three steps in this process are (1) assigning 3S job responsibilities, (2) integrating 3S duties into regular work duties, and (3) checking on the maintenance of the three pillars. When it comes to maintaining 3S conditions, everyone must know exactly what they are responsible for doing and exactly when, where, and how to do it. The five pillars must become part of the normal workflow. And 5S work must be brief, efficient, and habitual. Some of the tools used in making Sort, Set in Order, and Shine procedures a habit are 5S Job Cycle Charts, Visual 5S, 5-Minute 5S, a Standardization-Level Checklist, and 5S Checklists for healthcare facilities.

The second part of implementing the fourth pillar involves taking Standardize to the next level: prevention. Unbreakable standardization means making Sort, Set in Order, and Shine procedures unbreakable. The three aspects of unbreakable standardization are preventive Sort procedures, preventive Set in Order procedures, and preventive Shine procedures.

Preventive sorting means that instead of waiting until unneeded items accumulate, we find ways to prevent their accumulation. To do this, we must prevent unneeded items from even entering the workplace. Preventive setting in order means keeping the Set in Order procedures from breaking down. We do this by making it difficult or impossible to put things back in the wrong place. Several techniques for accomplishing this are the 5W1H Approach, Kitting, Incorporation, and Use Elimination. Finally, preventive shining means preventing things from becoming contaminated. The key to preventive shining is treating contamination problems at their source. The closer you can get to the source of contamination, the better you will be able to implement preventive shining.

REFLECTIONS

- What did you learn from reading this chapter that stands out as being particularly useful or interesting to you in healthcare?
- Do you have any questions about the topics presented in this chapter? If so, what are they?
- Are there any special obstacles to implementing the 5S methods described in this chapter in a healthcare setting?
- What information do you still need to fully understand the ideas presented?
- How can you get this information?
- Who do you need to involve in this process?

Chapter 7

The Fifth Pillar

Sustain

CONTENTS

7.1 EXPLANATION OF THE FIFTH PILLAR—SUSTAIN

7.1.1 Introduction

In Chapters 3 through 5, you learned the tools and techniques of the Sort, Set in Order, and Shine pillars. In Chapter 6, you learned how to standardize the implementation of these three pillars. But what good are standards and procedures without the discipline to follow them? This is where the fifth pillar comes in.

7.1.2 Definition of the Fifth Pillar

The fifth pillar is *Sustain.* In the context of the five pillars, Sustain means to make a habit of properly maintaining correct 5S procedures.

In your life in general, what do you mean when you talk about sustaining something? Usually, you think of it as drawing on something from inside yourself in order to maintain a course of action—even when forces in your life challenge this effort.

7.1.3 Problems Avoided by Implementing Sustain

Here are some of the things that happen in an organization when commitment to the five pillars is not sustained:

1. Unneeded items begin piling up as soon as sorting is completed (see Figure 7.1).
2. No matter how well Set in Order is planned and implemented, equipment and instruments do not get returned to their designated places after use.
3. No matter how dirty or contaminated workplaces and equipment become, cleaning is left to the housekeeping/environmental services team at the end of the day.

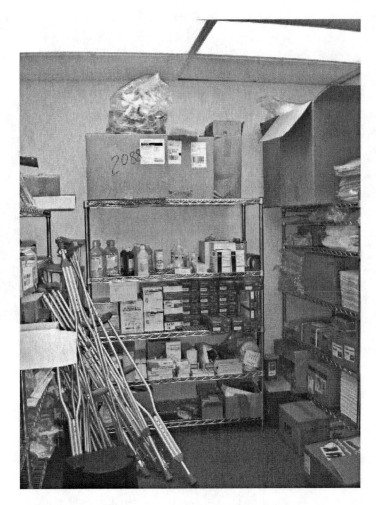

Figure 7.1   A disorderly medical supply room.

4. Providers believe they are too busy for "instant housekeeping" activities that help prevent hospital-acquired infections.
5. Equipment is left protruding into hallways, causing patients and providers to occasionally trip and get injured.
6. Dark, dirty, and disorganized workplaces lower patient and provider morale.

These 5S-related problems and others are likely to occur in any organization that lacks a commitment to sustain the five pillar gains over time.

Figure 7.2 Contemplating on the rewards of sustaining behavior.

7.1.4 Why Sustain Is Important

Key Point

Example

Usually, you commit yourself to sustain a particular course of action because the rewards for keeping to the course of action are greater than the rewards for departing from it (see Figure 7.2). Viewed another way, the consequences of not keeping to the course of action may be greater than the consequences of keeping to it.

For example, suppose you want to start an exercise program—say you decide you want to work out at a gym three times a week. You probably have difficulty sustaining this course of action. This is because forces in your life, such as limits on your time and energy, as well as the power of inertia, challenge this plan. However, if the rewards of sticking to your exercise program (e.g., feeling and looking better) are greater than the rewards of not sticking to it (e.g., having more time for other things that you need to do), your commitment will increase and you will probably sustain this program over time.

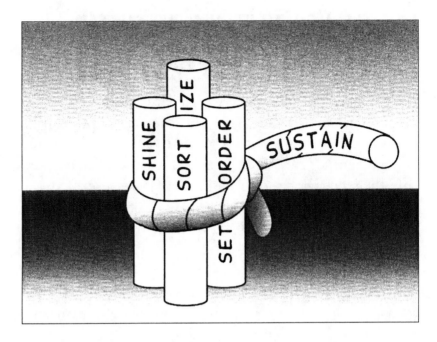

Figure 7.3 The Sustain pillar holds the first four pillars together.

Key Point The same principle applies in your 5S implementation. Without your commitment to sustain the benefits of the 5S activities, implementation of the first four pillars quickly falls apart (see Figure 7.3). However, if the rewards of implementing the first four pillars are greater for you than the rewards of not implementing them, sustaining them through the fifth pillar should be something you take to naturally.

So, what are the rewards for you of implementing the first four pillars? You have probably discovered them for yourself at this point. Implementation of the first four pillars should make your workplace more pleasant to work in, your job more satisfying, and communication with your fellow providers easier. It should also make your work more efficient and of better quality. It should also help you pass your Joint Commission or state health department accreditation surveys without the usual stress.

It is true that the five pillars take time to implement, but this investment of time will bring a great return, for you personally and for your organization.

7.2 HOW TO IMPLEMENT SUSTAIN

7.2.1 Creating Conditions to Sustain Your Plans

The implementation of the Sustain pillar is different from that of the Sort, Set in Order, Shine, or Standardize pillar in the sense that results are not visible and cannot be measured. Commitment to it exists in people's hearts and minds, and only their behavior shows its presence. Because of this, it cannot exactly be "implemented" like a technique. However, we can create conditions that encourage the implementation of the Sustain pillar.

For instance, going back to our exercise program example, how could you create conditions in your own life that would encourage sustaining your plan to work out at a gym three times a week? You might:

- Join a gym with a friend so you can work out together and encourage each other (see Figure 7.4).
- Create a workout schedule with your friend.
- Make a plan with your spouse to eat dinner later three nights a week so you can go to the gym after work.

Figure 7.4 Creating the conditions to sustain your fitness plan.

- Get extra sleep on the nights before you work out, so that you will not be too tired by the end of the day to follow through with your exercise plan.

These conditions would make it easier for you to sustain your schedule of exercising at the gym three times a week.

Key Point Similarly, you and your organization can create conditions or structures that will help sustain a commitment to the five pillars. The types of conditions that are most useful for this are:

- *Awareness.* You and your fellow providers need to understand what the five pillars are and how important it is to sustain them.
- *Time.* You need to have or make enough time in your work schedule to perform 5S implementation.
- *Structure.* You need to have a structure for how and when 5S activities will be implemented.
- *Support.* You need to have support for your efforts from management, in terms of acknowledgment, leadership, and resources.
- *Rewards and recognition.* Your efforts need to be rewarded.
- *Satisfaction and excitement.* The implementation of the five pillars needs to be fun and satisfying for you and the organization. This feeling of excitement and satisfaction gets communicated from person to person, allowing 5S implementation to build as it involves more people.

TAKE FIVE

Take 5 minutes to think about this question and jot down your answer:

- What are some conditions that would help sustain people's commitment to 5S implementation in your workplace?

7.2.2 Roles in Implementation

Key Point

To sustain 5S implementation in your organization, both you and your organization's management have important roles to play. These roles involve creating the conditions that sustain 5S activities and demonstrating a commitment to 5S.

7.2.2.1 The Role of Management

The supervisors and managers in your organization have a major role to play in ensuring the success of the five pillars by creating conditions that help sustain 5S activities. This role includes:

- Educating yourself and your fellow providers about 5S concepts, tools, and techniques
- Creating teams for implementation
- Empowering the frontline staff to make substantive changes in their work
- Allowing time for implementation and creating schedules for this work
- Providing resources for 5S implementation, such as supplies
- Acknowledging and supporting 5S efforts
- Encouraging creative involvement by all providers and staff, listening to their ideas, and acting on them
- Creating both tangible and intangible rewards for 5S efforts
- Acknowledging and rewarding staff who embrace the five pillars
- Promoting ongoing 5S efforts
- Being present in the workplace to observe the work being done

Your supervisors and managers also have an important role to play in implementing the fifth pillar in their own work. When they sustain the first four pillars, they perform three very important functions:

- Improving the quality and efficiency of their own work

- Teaching by example
- Demonstrating the organization's commitment to 5S implementation

7.2.2.2 Your Role

Similarly, you have an important role to play in creating the conditions that sustain 5S activities. This role includes the following:

- Continuing to learn more about 5S implementation
- Helping educate your fellow providers about the 5S
- Being enthusiastic about 5S implementation
- Helping promote 5S implementation efforts

You also have an important role to play in order to sustain 5S activities in your own work. This role includes:

- Taking the initiative to figure out ways to implement the five pillars in your work on a daily basis
- Asking your supervisor or manager for the support or resources you need to implement the five pillars
- Participating fully in your organization's 5S implementation efforts
- Bringing to your supervisor or manager your creative ideas for promoting or implementing the five pillars
- Participating fully in your organization's 5S promotion efforts (see Figure 7.5)

7.3 TOOLS AND TECHNIQUES TO SUSTAIN 5S IMPLEMENTATION

 There are many tools and techniques your organization can use to help sustain commitment to 5S implementation. We discuss them below so you will be aware of them. At some point in your 5S implementation work, you may be called upon to use or even coordinate the use of these techniques.

Figure 7.5   Enthusiasm for 5S implementation.

7.3.1 5S Slogans

New Tool

5S Slogans communicate the themes of the 5S campaign in your organization. They are most effective when they are suggested by you and your fellow providers. They can be displayed on buttons, stickers, flags, or posters.

7.3.2 5S Posters

Posters displaying 5S Slogans or descriptions of 5S activities can be posted throughout the workplace. They can serve to remind everyone of the importance of the five pillars or to communicate the results or status of 5S activities.

7.3.3 5S Photo Exhibits and Storyboards

When it comes to communication about 5S implementation, the old saying that a "picture is worth a thousand words" is definitely true. Photo exhibits and storyboards showing the "before" and "after" of 5S implementation activities are powerful tools for promoting the five pillars. Photos and storyboards can also communicate the status of 5S activities.

7.3.4 5S Newsletters

New Tool

5S Newsletters are in-house news bulletins centered on 5S topics. They carry reports on 5S conditions and activities. 5S Newsletters are most effective when issued on a regular basis, perhaps once or twice a month and at staff meetings.

7.3.5 5S Maps

5S Maps can also be used to get employees involved in 5S improvement on an ongoing basis (see Figure 7.6). 5S Improvement Maps should be hung in a central location with suggestion cards attached so anyone can suggest improvements.

7.3.6 5S Pocket Manuals

A 5S Pocket Manual can be created that contains 5S definitions and descriptions and is small enough to fit into the

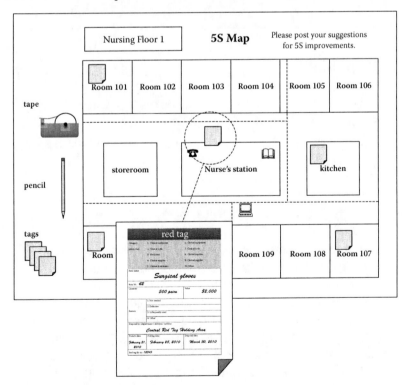

Figure 7.6   5S Map used to gather improvement suggestions.

pocket of your scrubs. Healthcare providers, supervisors, and managers can all use 5S Pocket Manuals for easy reference to the 5S essentials.

7.3.7 5S Department Tours

When one department in an organization has implemented the five pillars successfully, it can serve as a model area for other departments to come visit. Since "seeing is believing," this technique is extremely effective for promoting 5S implementation throughout an organization.

TAKE FIVE

Take 5 minutes to think about this question and jot down your answer.

- What are some other ideas of how you might promote 5S activities in your workplace? Name at least three.

7.3.8 5S Months

Organizations should designate 2, 3, or 4 months every year as "5S Months." During these months, various activities such as 5S seminars, field trips, and contests can be carried out to further promote 5S implementation in the organization.

SUMMARY

The fifth pillar, Sustain, means to make a habit of properly maintaining correct procedures over time. No matter how well implemented the first four pillars are, the 5S system will not work for long without a commitment to sustain it.

In your life in general, why do you commit yourself to sustain a particular course of action? Usually, you do this because the rewards of keeping to the course of action are greater than the rewards of departing from it. Similarly, if

---

the rewards of implementing the five pillars are greater for you than the rewards of not implementing them, sustaining them through the fifth pillar should be something you take to naturally.

Unlike the first four pillars, the Sustain pillar cannot be implemented by a set of techniques, nor can it be measured easily. However, you and your organization can create conditions or structures that will help sustain the commitment to 5S implementation.

To sustain 5S activities in your organization, both you and your organization's management have important roles to play. These roles involve creating the conditions that sustain 5S activities and demonstrating that you are committed to sustain these activities, personally. Some of the tools to help sustain 5S activities in your organization include 5S Slogans, 5S Posters, 5S Photo Exhibits and Storyboards, 5S Newsletters, 5S Pocket Manuals, 5S Department Tours, and 5S Months.

REFLECTIONS

- What did you learn from reading this chapter that stands out as being particularly useful or interesting to you in healthcare?
- Do you have any questions about the topics presented in this chapter? If so, what are they?
- Are there any special obstacles to implementing the 5S methods described in this chapter in a healthcare setting?
- What information do you still need to fully understand the ideas presented?
- How can you get this information?
- Who do you need to involve in this process?

Chapter 8

Reflections and Conclusions

CONTENTS

8.1 REFLECTING ON WHAT YOU HAVE LEARNED

Key Point

An important part of learning is reflecting on what you have learned. Without this step, learning cannot take place effectively. Now that you have come to the end of this book, we would like to ask you to reflect on what you have learned. We suggest you take 10 minutes to write down some quick answers to the following questions:

■ In Chapter 1, you considered the question, "What do I want to get out of reading this book?"
    – Have you gotten what you wanted to get out of this book?
    – Why or why not?

- What ideas, tools, and techniques that will be most useful in your own life, at work, or at home have you learned? How will they be useful?
- What ideas, tools, and techniques that will be least useful in your own life, at work, or at home have you learned? Why are they not useful?

8.2 APPLYING WHAT YOU HAVE LEARNED

8.2.1 Possibilities for Applying What You Have Learned

The way you decide to apply what you have learned will, of course, depend on your situation. If your organization is launching a full-scale 5S implementation program, you should have ample opportunity to apply what you have learned at work. In this case, you may be included in a team of people who are responsible for implementing the five pillars in a certain work area. You may have implementation time structured into your workday and may be responsible for reporting the results of your activities on a regular basis.

On the other end of the spectrum, your organization may have no immediate plan to implement the five pillars. In this case, the extent to which you can implement what you have learned will depend on how much control you have over your own schedule, workflow, and work area. However, you plan to apply what you have learned about the five pillars, a good place to start practicing 5S concepts and tools is at home. We have seen people who react to the learning presented in this book by spending an entire weekend applying the five pillars to a kitchen, clothes closet, or garage (see Figure 8.1). This, of course, may have its own limitations, since it is likely that your family has not read this book and may have questions about your 5S activities.

Figure 8.1 Practicing the Shadow-Boarding strategy at home.

8.2.2 Implementing 5S in Your Organization

Because the 5S's appear to be simple on the surface (we have seen that they are not), some managers mistakenly assume that implementation is also simple. As we have already mentioned, a successful 5S program requires top management participation. You also need the right organization. Figure 8.2 describes a 5S Council, which includes 5S promoters from all management levels, from the president down through the departments (Departments X, Y, and Z) and all the way to the supervisory level (Sections A, B, and C). This council has the ultimate decision-making authority regarding the delegation of duties concerning the 5S campaign. The 5S Council also formulates policies regarding various 5S activities, plans the 5S activity calendar, and provides general implementation instructions. The 5S Promotion Council is a small team of 5S Council members who work out the details of planned 5S activities and provide explicit instructions and encouragement to make 5S implementation go more smoothly on the shop floor.

In addition to the right organization, you will need a detailed implementation plan. Figure 8.3 shows how you might plan an implementation focused on the first three pillars. This plan

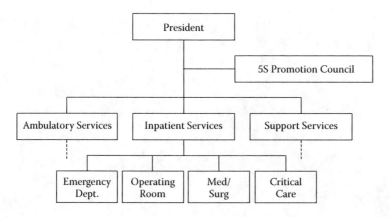

Figure 8.2 5S council.

In-house Promotion Schedule for 5S Campaign

Schedule creation date:_____

Site: _____

A. Names of 5S Campaign Participants

		Person responsible	Action date	To be done by
B. Preparation Jan. 25-29	1) Explain the 5Ss at an all-employee meeting.			
	2) Make provisional list of red-tag targets.			
C. Implementation Feb. 1-12	1) Complete red tag strategy implementation plan.			
	2) Form red tag team.			
	3) Red-tag unneeded items.			
	4) Catalogue red-tagged items.			
	5) Cull returnable purchased items from red-tagged items.			
	6) Make list of returnable purchased items.			
	7) Return purchased items.			
Feb. 17-22	8) Move red-tagged items to red tag holding area.			
	9) Confirm completion of tasks 1-8.			
	10) Identify locations for needed items.			
	11) Create location indicators for needed items.			
	12) Create amount indicators for needed items.			
	13) Install location and amount indicators.			
	14) Create signboards.			
	15) Put up signboards.			
	16) Confirm completion of tasks 13-14.			
	17) Set up Cleanliness tools and implement S3.			
	18) Maintain Cleanliness.			
	18) Confirm completion of all of the tasks listed above.			
Feb. 22-28	20) 5S Council members carry out 5S patrols.			
D. Results compilation Mar. 1-5	1) Make in-house management chart of red-tagged items.			
	2) Send management chart to 5S Promotion Office.			
Mar. 7-20	3) Collect companywide data at 5S Promotion Office.			

Figure 8.3 In-house promotion schedule for a 5S campaign.

begins with the first pillar, Sort, by removing unneeded items and returning excess purchased items and then follows up with 5 days of intensive work on the second and third pillars, Set in Order and Shine. Note how the 5S Council members get involved later in 5S Audits. This is the fourth pillar in action, Standardize.

8.2.3 Your Personal Action Plan

Key Point

You may or may not be in a management position that permits you to plan 5S activity on a grand scale. Whatever your situation, we suggest you create a personal action plan for how you will begin applying the information you have learned from this book. You might start by referring to your own notes about the tools and techniques you think will be most useful to you and then write down answers to the following questions:

- What can I implement right now at work that will make my job easier, better, or more efficient?
- What can I implement at home right now that will make activities there flow more easily or more efficiently?
- How can I involve others at home and at work in the implementation of what I have learned?

When you have answered these questions, we suggest that you commit to completing the things you have written down in a specific period and to making a new plan at the end of that period.

Key Point

It is often good to start with something small that you can comfortably finish in the time you have allowed yourself. If the project is too ambitious or time consuming, you can easily get discouraged and might give up.

Key Point

Also, projects you can work on for short periods whenever you get a chance are ideal in the beginning. For example, you might decide to reorganize a storage area, one set of shelves at a time, in 5- or 10-minute chunks.

8.3 OPPORTUNITIES FOR FURTHER LEARNING

Here are some ways to learn more about the five pillars:

- Find other books or videos on this subject. Several of these are listed on the next page.
- If your organization is already implementing the five pillars, visit other departments to see how they are using 5S tools and techniques.
- Find out how other healthcare organizations have implemented the five pillars.
- Consider visiting local manufacturing companies with successful 5S implementations.

8.4 CONCLUSIONS

The 5S approach is a simple but powerful method for improvement in the healthcare environment. We hope this book has given you a taste of how this method can be helpful and effective for you in your work. Productivity Press and the Rona Consulting Group welcome your stories about how you apply the five pillars in your own workplace.

FURTHER READING ABOUT THE 5S SYSTEM

The following resources, available from Productivity Press, will provide you with additional education about various aspects of the 5S system:

Productivity Press Development Team, ed., *5 Pillars of the Visual Workplace* (Productivity Press, 1995)—This is the sourcebook for *5S for Healthcare*. It includes case studies, numerous illustrations, and detailed information about how to initiate and manage a 5S implementation effort in any organization.

M. Grief, *The Visual Factory: Building Participation Through Shared Information* (Productivity Press, 1991)—This book shows how visual management techniques can provide "just-in-time" information to support teamwork and employee participation.

N. K. Shimbun, ed., *Visual Control Systems* (Productivity Press, 1995)—This book presents articles and case studies that detail how visual control systems have been implemented in a variety of organizations.

FURTHER READING ABOUT LEAN HEALTHCARE

M. Graban, *Lean Hospitals: Improving Quality, Patient Safety, and Employee Satisfaction* (New York: Productivity Press, 2009)—This book explains why and how *lean* can be used to improve quality, safety, and morale in a healthcare setting. Graban highlights the benefits of lean methods and explains how lean manufacturing staples, such as Value Stream Mapping, can help hospital personnel identify and eliminate waste, effectively preventing delays for patients, reducing wasted motion for caregivers, and improving quality of care.

N. Grunden, *The Pittsburgh Way: Improving Patient Care Using Toyota Based Methods* (New York: Productivity Press, 2008)—Grunden provides a hopeful look at how principles borrowed from industry can be applied to make healthcare safer and, in doing so, make it more efficient and less costly. The book is a compilation of case studies from units in different hospitals around the Pittsburgh region that successfully applied industrial principles, making patients safer and employees more satisfied.

J. C. Bauer & Mark Hagland, *Paradox and Imperatives in Health Care: How Efficiency, Effectiveness, and E-Transformation Can Conquer Waste and Optimize Quality* (New York: Productivity Press, 2008). Bauer and Hagland explain why providers must draw upon internal resources to increase net revenue and provide the quality of care that payers and consumers are demanding. Through numerous case studies, the authors show how pioneering healthcare organizations are using performance improvement tools—including lean management, Six Sigma, and the Toyota Production System—to produce excellent services as inexpensively as possible.

USEFUL WEB SITES

Lean Blog—Founded by Mark Graban, this blog is about *lean* in factories, hospitals, and the world around us (http://www .leanblog.org/).

Lean Healthcare Grand Rounds—A blog for lean thinkers who are transforming healthcare with the Toyota Management System (http://leangrandrounds.blogspot.com).

John Grout's Mistake-Proofing Center—Shingo Prize winner John Grout's collection of three web sites devoted to *poka yoke* (mistake proofing), a key technique for 5S and lean operations generally. An entire web site within the center is devoted to healthcare applications of mistake proofing (http://www .mistakeproofing.com).

http://www.ronaconsulting.com—The official web site of series editor Thomas L. Jackson and his partners at the Rona Consulting Group.

http://www.productivitypress.com—The web site of Productivity Press, where you may order the books mentioned above, among many others, about lean manufacturing, total quality management, and total productive maintenance.

Index

U

Unbreakable sorting, 90
Unbreakable standardization, 89, 90
Unneeded items
  accumulation, 42–43
  types, 42
Unsafe conditions waste, 49
Use elimination, 94–95

V

Vertical address, 57
Visual controls, 49–50
Visual 5S, 85–86, 97
Visually identifying locations, 56
Visual setting in order, 62

W

Waiting patients, 23, 25
Waiting room, 97

Waste, 48
  accumulation, 16
  defects, 49
  example, 16–17
  excess inventory, 49
  human energy, 49
  medical, 66, 89
  motion, 48
  searching, 48
  unsafe conditions, 49
Websites, 120
Work environment, 27
Workflow, 31
Workplace, 103
  design, 23
  employee morale, 27
  Hirano's system, 6
  organization, 6

Z

Zero delays for deliveries, 25

Author

Thomas L. Jackson, JD, MBA, PhD, is the former CEO of Productivity, Inc., and Productivity Press, and a member of the influential Ford Lean Advisory Group. Tom has been a student of lean enterprise since 1988, when he copyedited Hiroyuki Hirano's *JIT Factory Revolution* for Productivity Press and reworked two chapters of Yasuhiro Monden's groundbreaking *Japanese Management Accounting*. Looking at pictures of Japanese factories and reading about how differently the Japanese count their money, Tom became so fanatical about lean that he left his comfortable position as a professor of business at the University of Vermont to start his own lean consulting company—in Malaysia! There, he learned that the powerful techniques of lean enterprise— JIT, SMED, TPM, and kanban—were only half of the story of Toyota's great success. The other half of the story was *hoshin kanri* (a.k.a. the "balanced scorecard") and a revolution in the structure of modern business organization. In 2005, Tom started applying Toyota's operational and management methods in healthcare in a small rural clinic in Seward, Alaska. In 2008, Tom decided to trade his Levi's Dockers for a pair of black scrubs and joined Mike Rona, former president of Seattle's Virginia Mason Medical Center, as a partner in the Rona Consulting Group, where he and Mike are "transforming healthcare and pursuing perfection." In 2007, Tom was awarded a Shingo Prize for his book, *Hoshin Kanri for the Lean Enterprise*. In 2009, Tom was appointed Clinical Associate Professor in the Department of Health Services of the University of Washington's School of Public Health.